PREFACE.

I<small>F</small> round the hearths in Winter,
　Or in Autumnal days,
In the leisure hours of toilers,
　Should be read these rugged lays,
These tales of Races sunk away
　In Time's unfathomed haze ;
May they please the gracious readers,
　And the audience that hears ;
May they picture to the fancy
　In far-receding years
The lives of grey forefathers—
　Old forefathers of the Drift,
Old Cave men, and old huntsmen
　With spear and arrow swift ;
May they pass in open vision
　As scenes that shift and shift
On the wide stage of human life ;
　That who attends may know
From the first unto the latest day,
　The stream of life doth flow—
That we are here because they lived
　In ages long ago.

The Seven Sagas Of Prehistoric Man

James Hastie Stoddart

THE SEVEN SAGAS

OF

PREHISTORIC MAN

BY

JAMES H. STODDART

AUTHOR OF "THE VILLAGE LIFE"

𝔏𝔬𝔫𝔡𝔬𝔫

CHATTO AND WINDUS, PICCADILLY

1884

TO

MRS. JOHN CAMERON,

A SINCERE AND KIND

FRIEND,

I INSCRIBE THIS VOLUME.

J. H. S.

CONTENTS.

THE EARLIEST MAN.

B

THE EARLIEST MAN.

A FLINT flake, rudely edged ; you might
    Impatient pass it by,
And wonder why illustrious men
    Should turn it curiously,
And gaze with reverence on it
    As if its worth were high.

A common piece of flint it seems,
    Torn from its parent bed,—
The mountain limestone—by a stream
    That through the valley sped,
And swirled the fragment to the shore,
    At a long level head.

That flint is the divinest stone
    That human eyes may scan,
For on its edge is written deep
    An Apocalypse of man.
In the remote millenniums,
    Before our rivers ran
Their ancient courses, and before
    Our present sea swept round

The green isle of the Celtic West;
  Before the ocean found
And formed the stormy channel
  Between French and British ground,—
A man's hand held the flint flake,
  And chipped it till a blade,
Keen as an edge of iron,
  Killed, cut, and scraped and flayed;
The noblest weapon of its day
  By human fingers made.

Who taught him to observe the flint,
  And mark the cleavings keen?
Who taught him that a cutting edge
  The cleavings lay between?
High Reason, lord of brutes, alone
  Taught man in the remote
And long forgotten ages,
  To shape his work by thought,
And to reason out a weapon
  On a plan that brutes had not,
And to use it for a purpose
  When he hunted or he fought.

Half-human sire of every race
  In all the lands that be,
That oldest worker on the flints
  Evades our scrutiny.

Whence came he, and from what emerged?
　What was his ancestry?

Dark as the realms of Yama
　Our Aryan fathers feared,
Dark as the steaming globe was once,
　Before the sun appeared,
And with its fervent light and heat ·
　A brood of life upreared,—
Thus dark is the life vision,
　That on this edge of flint
Reveals, and but reveals a man,
　Who left his large imprint
Of life and reason on it,
　But beyond no further glint.

We figure him a savage,
　With hands to rudely shape
A weapon for his uses;
　Low-templed like the ape,
With large projecting eyebrows,
　And jaws that widely gape,
With hairy hide, unclad, or clad
　In winter with the skin
Of some fierce brute his cunning caught
　By stealthy stalk or gin,
Or by a happy blow of club,
　That to the brain broke in.

Ages before this flint was worked
　His sires had led their lives
In savage misery in the woods;
　And with their dusky wives
Reared dusky children; but no trace
　Of that dark age survives.
Yet they had found the secret
　To kindle from the dead,
Dry, withered leaves and branches
　A night-fire, shooting red
Within its smoke, and lighting round
　The cave or forest bed.

And farther distant in the past,
　Before the Drift man rose,
An ancient father wandered,
　And battled with his foes.
And still before this ancient man
　An older had his close
Of savage life, of fear and joy.
　And backward we may wend,
By fancy only guided,
　To some far distant end,
When with the Inarticulate
　The sires of mankind blend.

But who can trace the long descent?
  Who reckon up the sum
Of structure and of tendencies,
  That from the creature dumb
And forest-roving might be built
  The form from which should come
The speaking tribes of mankind,—
  Drift fathers long ago,
Dim fathers of the human time?
  There is no highest glow
Of most excelling genius
  That to the world can show
A light behind the dark that veils
  This Stone—the earliest spark
Of human effort in the world,
  The first touch and the mark
Of mind above the brutish mind,
  The first gleam from the dark
Of an intelligence above
  All that had ever been
Since earth was earth, and creatures lived,
  Since trees were high and green;
Here first is a reflecting man,
  Revealed upon the scene.

This old man lived by river banks
  In the short winter days;

Secure in deep-worn caves he slept,
  And by his wood-fire's blaze,
Ate, drank, and danced until the rage
  Of hunger, many ways
Sent him forth roaming with his wives;
  A hunter, cunning, bold.
And in the summer time he made
  His home within the wold,
Beneath a great-limbed leafy tree;
  At sundown he would fold
His family, and till the dawn
  Keep living the red flame,
That warmed his young and scared away
  The things of evil fame,
And terrified the giant brutes
  That round his lodging came.

Low, mean, and savage life was his,
  A life of evil fare.
His food was always hard to find,
  Though it was all his care,
And hunger often forced him
  A cruel fate to dare.
If luck had sent him rowth of food,
  He feasted all the day,
And slept and feasted till his stores
  Had all been swept away,

And till the pangs of hunger came,
  Brute satisfied he lay.

A wary, cunning soul was his ;
  Though all but weaponless,
He toiled and planned, and snared and caught,
  With knowledge and finesse.
He studied haunts and habitats,
  And customs of the wild ;
The times of all the beasts he knew,
  And all he had beguiled.
With quick wit he had watched them
  Since he had been a child.

His ancestors had left him,
  Besides his instincts strong,
Destructive, and lascivious,
  A glint of right and wrong,
Of tribal justice and of laws ;
  He had his moral code,
And solemn forms of social life
  With friends and foes abroad ;
He was human at the highest,
  Though the brute within him glowed.

All this the flint flake teaches
  To the instructed eye ;

And beside this rudest weapon
  Many other relics lie
In the ancient Drift to teach us;
  And they speak with certainty
Of the age and its surroundings;
  Of the animals that shared
The forest with him and the cave;
  And the relics Time has spared,
People again this older world,
  Sunk deep beneath the old;
The aided vision through the dusk
  May dimly still behold,
On the great plains, and swamps, and woods,
  And on the ranges bold,
Upland and mountain, creatures strange;
  Though few of them remain,
Some changed in structure, many lost,
  And some driven back again
To other wilds, in lordly pride
  Predominant to reign.

Here with the early Drift man roamed
  The Mammoth, lord of brutes
In bulk and strength; his mighty tusks
  Curved upward from their roots;
He trampled through the forest depth,
  And fed on the green shoots.

And in the deep broad rivers
　　The Sea Bull reared his head,
Snorting with pleasure as he rose
　　And on the green banks fed.
And the grisly bear in winter
　　In the caves hybernated.

At dusk the Sabre Tooth stole out
　　From cave or thorny brake—
Our tiger with a stronger jaw
　　And of a mightier make,
And fiercer temper; when he snarled
　　His savage lips would peel
O'er flashing tusks, like the fell edge
　　Of swords of tempered steel;
And when he roared, the forest shook
　　As from a thunder peal.

Huge shouldered, and low hipped, and high,
　　Above the grass he strode,
Light on his foot, and yet his paw
　　Fell like the bolt of God,
And tore down to the bones the brute
　　On which he laid his load.
The Mammoth shunned him, for his strength
　　Availed not in the fight

When rending paw and flashing teeth
  And muscles twitching tight,
Opposed the sluggish monster,
  Without vigour with his might.

Oft in his cave the Drift man heard
  The forest glades resound
With the low growlings in his rage,—
  Mouth sweeping on the ground,—
Of the Dread Cruelty that stalked
  His blazing wood-fire round.

He heard him and revered him,
  No brute more feared than he;
But though the old man feared him,
  He trapped him subtlely,
And stripped him of his tawny hide
  With taunting words and glee.

And the Rhinoceros afar
  In gloomy fens made lair,
The snub-nosed and the woolly-skinned,
  Caught sometimes in the snare
Of the wily forest-hunter,
  Who picked his great bones bare.
The mottled-skinned Hyæna yelped
  In packs within the glade,

Following fast the Sabre Tooth
  Upon his murderous raid;
Or prowled around the camp-fire
  The Drift man's wives had made.

Great herds of bison crossed the plains
  And fed on springing grass,
They came in thousands leisurely,
  Through the time-trodden pass;
And he took toll of them at the fords,
  As they struggled mass on mass.

The elk, with mighty antlers
  Spread broad above his head,
And fierce kine, roaming through the wilds,
  Not yet subdued and bred,
And the unmounted horse that fleet
  Before pursuers fled,
Were all the huntsman's quarry;
  He cared not but to slay,
And stock his cave or forest hut
  With fresh meat day by day.

His weapons :—heavy club of oak,
  A scraping disc of flint,
A heavy axe by nature formed—
  A round quartz with the print

Of effort on its thinner end,
   To give it cutting edge—
By the thick round he held it,
   He knew not how to wedge
The stone into a handle;
   And of other weapons none,
But from the wild beasts of the field
   His food was daily won.
He sowed no seeds, and in his days
   The forest fruits were few.
The oak tree yielded acorns,
   And wild roots he could chew
He found among the grasses;
   And from the stream he drew
By wile and gin the scaly tribe;
   But from the rivers broad,
And from the wide shores of the sea,
   He little sustenance owed;
The art of shaping out a boat
   Had not yet been bestowed.

Shell-fish he found upon the shore,
   And at the spawning time,
When shoals of salmon crowded round
   The linns they strove to climb,
He caught and feasted on them;
   And the wreckage of the plains,

Of the forests and the mountains,
  He tracked the lost remains.

He knew where fell the rutting buck ;
  He found the crippled doe,
And he watched the calving kine, and stole
  The young ones while they low,
In piteous plaint, upon their dams,
  For ruth he did not know.

Single-handed all his woodcraft,
  All his hunting, had been vain
And feeble, as against the brutes
  That kept the mount and plain,
And were masters of the forest depths,
  Before he dared to reign.

But kindred families had grown
  Into a social band,
A little tribe and commune,
  Who worked with common hand,
And hunted for each other's need,
  Under the sole command
Of a brave crafty leader,
  Experienced in the field.
His was the right to guide them,
  When round the evening bield
A ravenous brute sent forth a voice
  That through the forest pealed.

And when a hostile tribe burst in
    Upon their hunting-ground,
His club was always first in hand,
    And in the front was found;
His terror-dealing blows were first
    To meet th' intruding race.
He ruled by strength and courage
    And endurance in the chase;
And when at last by club, or stone,
    Or age he lost his place,
The strongest man succeeded him.
    And after him there rose,
Out of the many chieftains
    Renowned for fighting foes,
Still wiser, fiercer, stronger men:
    Men overruling those—
Great heroes and great hunters,
    Who taught with higher skill,
The tribes to hunt with better craft,
    With finer flints to kill;

Great men in prehistoric time,
    In olden lands afar,
Old Nimrods, Cæsars, Charlemagnes
    In hunting and in war,
With names above all other names,
    And glorious as the star

That led the Drift man to his wives.
  But all forgotten they,
Although mayhap revered as gods,
  To whom the Drift men may
Have paid their homage, if had dawned
  A dim religious ray
Upon their brutish souls ; but now,
  All dust they are, and gone,
And long before the memory
  The modern race can own,
Aught but the recent heroes,
  That recent myths have grown—
A narrow life of mankind—
  These earlier lives were led,
Far in the past dim ages,
  Uncounted of the dead.

Yet through the darkness, thick and deep,
  Historic, there is shed,   '
On the back-gazing eye, a light,
  Revealing many a gift
To mankind from those heroes,
  Who in the ancient Drift
Had name and fame and genius,
  Swept up into the lift.

And this the flint flake teaches,
  Sole relic of a race

C

Dead, buried in alluvial depths,
    Its far-off resting-place ;
For not dubious or uncertain,
    Man then lived with subtle brain ;
Lived and hunted, loved and hated,
    And o'er the world's domain,
His lordship by his soul alone
    Victorious did maintain.

He ranged from the great tablelands
    Beyond the Caspian Sea ;
Far in the East and in the West
    No break or stop had he.
Our world is new compared with his,—
    New islands and new shores,
New rivers and new seas are ours,
    New beings, ampler stores
Of food for man and creature—
    All things have been made new ;
A fresher and a lovelier world
    Is now within our view.

And from this rudely fashioned flint,
    So old ! in time has grown,
By slow endeavour of the race,
    All weapons that we own—
All tools ; the great machinery
    That links us zone with zone.

In this frayed chip that bears the mark
    Of a primeval hand,
The newer man, with eyes to see
    And soul to understand,
May see and dimly reckon up
    The stages sure and grand,
In the wide stretch of time between
    The ancient hand and mind,
And the last touch of skill in work
    The last thought has defined,
In the lustrous strength of reason,
    By the genius of our kind.

For all our work, our highest soul,
    Is present in the face
Of this old weapon, thrown aside
    By a half-human race,
In darkest prehistoric time,
    At its last resting-place.

THE CAVE MAN.

THE CAVE MAN.

Long reaches down the stream of time,
  The Drift man disappears;
How? why? or where? is all unknown—
  He had fulfilled his years.
And a new man succeeded him,
  With arrows and with spears—
A savage man, a hunter,
  Who knew not yet to till
The fertile breast of Mother Earth,
  And from her increase fill
His ancient home with peaceful food;
  Yet with increasing skill,
He better knew to chip the flint,
  And fix it to a dart;
He had discovered, or had brought
  From some remoter part,
The bow and arrows, instrument
  Of more destructive art.

Unseen he stood and drew his bow
  And struck his quarry down,

And even monsters of the plain,
  When many shafts had flown,
Fell before repeated blows
  Of a foe that stood unknown.

This ancient man had nimble hands,
  As many a relic shows.
His tools and arms of flint and bone,
  To hunt, or to oppose
His savage neighbours, were devised
  With a true glimpse of taste.
He with an artist's eye and skill,
  Selecting from the waste
Of bone, and horn, and mighty tusk,
  That round his Cave were placed,
Shaped out bold weapon handles,
  And on their smoothness traced,
In flowing lines, artistic thoughts ;—
  The young deer, fighting strong
And overmastering the buck,
  That had for seasons long,
Taken his choice of nimble does,
  And stalked with pride among.

And the Mammoth, standing deep in grass,
  With meditative eye,
Or charging wildly open-mouthed,
  And trumping trunk on high,

His gleaming tusks revealing
    A foe was lurking nigh.

The horse, he pictured pleasantly,
    And archer keen at hand,
Fitting his arrow to the string,
    Prepared to launch the wand,
Flint-pointed, at the noble brute
    Men did not yet command.

And pictures of the seal he scraped
    With his flint-burin, clear
Upon the polished bone, his prey,
    In the long winters drear;
He speared him at the river mouth,
    Or by the white seas near.

We see him at his Cave home,
    And round about it spread
The refuse of his housekeeping,
    The brown skulls of his dead;
We watch him by the night fire,
    With wives and children there;
His sons, their wives, and grandsons,
    All working in the glare
Of the pine-light shooting upward
    Into the evening air;

And their shadows glimmer backward
   In the forest by their side.
Some are scraping with the flint flakes
   The Mammoth's hairy hide;
Some are forming a new weapon
   That another tribe has tried;

And others cut young branches
   Until they deftly grow,
By labour of the workmen's hand,
   Into a shapely bow.
And maidens point the arrow-heads,
   Before them in a row,
With jagged flints and points of bone;
   And little children ply
The light flints on the whetstone,
   Or mischievously try
To pick the meat from off the fire
   When the elders are not nigh.

In the fire-glow sits the artist,
   With bone blade on his knee,
Tracing with his pen of flint,
   In flowing lines and free,
The last achievement of the tribe,
   Won by its energy.

The feast is shared around the fire;
   Then another fire is lit.

Some paces nearer to the stream,
  Around the inner, sit—
The older men and women,—
  To give the dancers space
For the solemn dance to welcome
  The coming to the place
Of the great herds of bison,
  The vast migrating race,
Following the green pastures,
  And the instincts of their kind;
And the welcome dance has lasted
  Since time was out of mind.
And eagerly the dancers flit
  Between the glowing fires,
Young men, and wives, and maidens,
  Full of life and young desires,
Till passion, roused and heated,
  In violence expires.

But as the dance grew wilder,
  A growl, and then a roar,
Above the din and river rush,
  Were heard; and long before
The terror-stricken kinsmen
  Could fly, the shock was o'er.

A Sabre Tooth sprang light above
  The outer fire, and caught

Even as he fell a hunter brave,
　And with his fierce onslaught
Slew him and bore him swift away;
　And cat-like he withdrew,
With easy tread, beyond the light,
　Careless, as if he knew
That none would dare to follow him,
　And in revenge pursue.

The monster took the artist,
　The best man of the clan;
And a loud wail arose around,
　From woman and from man;
And fast into the Cave the braves,
　With furious outcries, ran.

They seized their weapons and rushed out,
　The old men bearing light.
They followed hard the bloody spoor
　Till the great brute came in sight;
Beyond the woodland on the plain
　His ravenous appetite
He crouching glutted; but the shouts
　Amazed him at his prey,
And raising up his gory jaws,
　And fixing, glowing, grey,
His hell eyes on the Cave folks,
　He bounded forth away.

And, terror-struck, they saw him pass,
  The mightiest of the field,
The iron-limbed and engine-jawed,
  That to no brute would yield;
For the greatest fell beneath his stroke,
  The Cave bear and the bull,
And Man, when his hot belly's rage
  The wild game could not cool;
King of the forest and the plain,
  None might dispute his rule.

Then home returned the Cave folk,
  To women shedding tears,
To wildest strains of anguish,
  With futile clash of spears.
The artist true had mourners
  For many coming years;

Not one of all the tribe but owned
  Some relic of his art:
Some nice-shaped hammer handle,
  Some horn, or pin, or dart,
With the graphic tracings on it,
  He only could impart.

But chief of all the mourners
  Was her who shared his bed,

In a deep nook within the Cave,—
　The wife that he had led
A captive from a far-off tribe,
　And by rude custom wed.

The fairest of the women,
　And loved by him alone,
Clove to him as the sinew
　Cleaves firmly to the bone;
And children fair she bore to him;
　And now her lord was gone.
Grief silenced her the while the noise
　Of ancient rites arose
Above her bowed head as she sat,
　And heard their mournful close.

Then rose she from her place obscure,
　Like a chief among his foes,
And by the fire-light raised her arm,
　And to the old men said—
"My love is by the Sabre Tooth
　Struck dead among the dead,
But I will wield his spear and be
　In the tribe's place instead.
None other shall I take to me;
　For who of all the race
Of the Cave folks can be to me
　Like him, of manliest face

And tenderest passion, urgent
  With modesty and grace ?
Grant me his place within the tribe,
  And ere to-morrow's sun
Has sunk behind the burning hills,
  Revile me, if but one
Of all the kinsfolk has secured
  More spoil than I have won."

Then strode she to the fire-glow,
  That o'er the old chiefs spread ;
Clean-limbed she was, and litheliness
  From ankle up to head,
Revealed its flowing curves and bends ;
  And the young men looked afraid—
She looked so strong and daring,
  And they knew she would not wed.

Then rose the father of the tribe,
  Grey-haired and feeble-eyed,
For many a toil he had endured,
  And many a battle tried,
And home from many a savage hunt
  Had come unsatisfied.
Long tracks of plain and forest,
  In youth he traversed o'er,
When from his father's tribe he fled,
  Pursued and punished sore,

With nothing but his bow and spear,
  And the wide world all before.

None matched him as a hunter,
  His arrow fled like light,
And struck with quivering motion
  Where'er he fixed his sight;
His spear sped when he threw it,
  And swerved not in its might.
And soon his prowess won him
  The fairest of the maids
Of all the tribes that lived within
  The far-extending glades;
And home he brought her to the Cave,
  The centre of his raids.

There reared he sons and daughters,
  And from their loins arose
A tribe of fame in hunting,
  Of terror to its foes.
The father's skill, the mother's grace,
  The children fair disclose—
The choicest tribe, none equalled it
  In all the regions round;
Its bows were of the toughest,
  Its arrows most renowned.

Arose the father, and he took
  The widow by the hand:

"Your claim," he said, "my daughter,
    We hardly understand ;
But I am old and I have seen,
    When I had firm command
Of tribes combined in former days,
    Ere yet my strength had failed,
Strange things to happen,—I have seen,
    Where strength has not availed,
The cunning of the woman win ;
    And where the warrior quailed,
The warrior's wife and daughter
    Strike victory home !

                        In olden days,
    When with me was my bride,
How I remember ! fondly she
    Stood firmly by my side,
And followed with unerring stroke,
    The stroke that I had tried.
My daughter, thou shalt surely go
    At rising of the sun.
Put on thy husband's glossy skins ;
    And when the day is done,
Come to me with the trophies
    These lovely arms have won."

So spake he ; and the kinsfolk
    Who listened by the fire,

D

Arose and shouted every one
    As 'twere their heart's desire ;
For well they knew the noble dame
    To great deeds would aspire.

The Cave slept as the widowed one
    Her husband's weapons laid
Before the hearth fire, and rejoiced
    The while, as she surveyed
Their strength, their polish, and their edge ;
    And to herself she said—
" None better are there in the land,
    And if my hand be true,
As erst it was in other days,
    Before my lord I knew,
I surely to the chief shall bring
    More than his common due."

She laid the weapons by her side,
    And by her children dreamed.
Short was her dream, for dawn appeared,
    And ere in thought she seemed
To stretch her limbs, a cry arose ;
    The eager huntsmen screamed—
" Awake ! awake ! the sun is up,
    And at the fords appear
The mighty herds, their hoofy tramp
    The listener may hear ;

They cross in thousands leisurely,
  And wander far and near."

The weaponed men all issued forth,
  The matron followed fast,
And through the woodlands to the fords
  In ordered march they passed;
Each slung his bow and gripped his spear
  All ready for a cast.

Down to the river, broad and wide,
  They travelled till they spied,
On mount, on plain, in open glade,
  The bison's matted hide;
Thousands on thousands ranged they
  In great troops, side by side.
They all turned to the river,
  And drank deep as they crossed.
The tribe moved forward, and each brave
  Found a convenient post,
By sedgy bank or bushy knoll
  Or trunk a storm had tossed;
Each shook his arrows from his belt,
  And laid his long bow down,
And as the great brutes waded,
  Each face showed, fell and brown,
Above its covert, and a spear
  From each right hand was thrown.

Many were pierced and felt the sting
  Of the keen jagged blade ;
The herds tramped on their sullen pace,
  Great herds, slow undismayed.
They fill the ford and trample down
  The wounded as they wade ;

Then as the throng grew denser,
  A shower of arrows flew.
Shower upon shower they fell, and filled
  The herds with terror new,
And in a wild stampede, the bulls
  Pressed the wide water through,
And snorting, rushed into the woods ;
  Followed, with tail on high,
The timorous females and their calves,
  With many a bleeding thigh ;
For the aim was at the youngest,
  The readiest to die.

Out in the forest stood the dame—
  So wished she to be placed—
Near to the ancient pitfall,
  Dug for the wild beasts chased ;
It lay with the great ford in line,
  And many a horn had graced

Its sunken depth, of deer and bull,
　　Of elk, and tusky boar;
And the huge Mammoth there was snared,
　　Although its walls he tore
With his curved tusks of ivory,
　　And through his trunk sonore,
Piped to his fellows; yet he fell
　　Prey to the Cave man's skill.
Club, spear, and arrow did, at last,
　　The work of death fulfil;
And many feasts were made of him
　　With joyance round the pit,
And fires were lighted by its side,
　　That red the dancers lit,
Illumining the banquets
　　Won by the Cave man's wit.

Near stood the matron, with a spear—
　　The best of all the clan—
Behind a pine tree, watching fast
　　The bison as they ran ;
And as a great bull passed her,
　　Her spear was in his neck,
And from the wound the flowing blood
　　His dew-lap did bedeck.
He paused, and shuddered as he stood ;
　　She with an arrow quick,

Struck deep into his flank ; he reared
   Then rushed, and stumbling fell
Into the snare prepared for him ;
   And many, she knew well,
Would follow blindly after
   The lord that bore the bell.

And joy was hers, the trap was full.
   Yet on the wild herd rushed ;
They trampled down the feeble brutes,
   And by her covert brushed,
Till, far upon the distant plain,
   Their thundering hoofs were hushed.

Twice only had she struck, and still
   Had weapons lying near.
Before she turned to join her folks,
   She poised another spear,
And waited for another bull,
   To end his fierce career.

Nor waited long ; with dripping hide,
   A sullen bull passed by,
A patriarch of the herd he seemed,
   Big in the neck and thigh.
With easy pace he walked, but watched,
   With a black glowing eye,

From side to side; and as she rose
　And launched with all her might
The tight spear from her shoulder,
　His dark eye caught her sight;
And down his huge head lowered,
　And his tail rose to its height.

The spear had only grazed the neck
　Beneath the matted mane,
It sped beyond the savage bull,
　And fastened in the plain.
He snorting, pawing on the ground,
　Charged; and she flew amain,
But grasped her bow and arrows,
　And fleet of foot she sped,
Not to the ford 'where succour was,
　But through the woodland glade :
She hoped in the thick underwood
　His charge would be misled.

But the bison followed on her flight
　With instinct keen and true,
And every turn and tack she made
　In his great rage he knew;
He tore through brake and thorny bush,
　With deep revenge in view.

She slid behind a mighty pine,
　And fitting to her bow

A choice flint arrow, drew it hard.
　　It smote his shoulder low;
And though the blood around the wound
　　Did in red volume flow,
He felt it as a thorny scratch
　　That tears his hairy hide
When through the wood he rushes,
　　With a fell foe by his side—
A keen-toothed enemy that springs
　　Where the field is clear and wide.

Again from the pine trunk she sped,
　　And fitting to the string,
Even as she fled, another shaft,
　　She wheeled as on the wing,
And struck him in the sinewy neck;
　　And from the purple spring
The arrow tapped, the blood rushed out,
　　And loud the monster roared,
As for a moment on his knees
　　He fell, and she implored
Her husband's shade to aid her flight
　　To her kinsfolk at the ford.

A moment only, and he charged,
　　His huge front bended low;
The fire had kindled in his eyes,
　　And blood and foam did flow,

From mouth and nostrils breathing hard;
  She strung upon her bow
Her only flake, and with an aim
  Unnerved she sought his eye;
And as the dart sang from her hand
  The maddened brute was nigh.
The aim was fair, for through the orb
  It pierced, and slanted by;

It missed the brain, but the sore wound,
  Stopped short his charging pace;
He bellowed, as the blood ran down
  His trembling nose and face;
And the brown widow slipped away
  To a safe hiding-place.

Home, laden with the hunter's spoil,
  The tribe came to the cave,
And wives and mothers and old men,
  And children of the brave,
Came forth to meet them joyously,
  And honour to them gave.

But while the feast was spread, the chief
  Looked round, and missed the fair
Brown huntress, who had tribal leave
  The perilous task to share

Of hunting the wild bison
  With her husband's bow and spear.
And he gloomed as he glanced round him,
  And his voice was raised above
The emulous tones of warriors,
  And the boisterous trills of love,
And the shouts of merry children,
  Who played around the fire,
And fed its flames to roast the food
  That roused their keen desire;

But the voice of the old chieftain,
  The high commanding sire,
Hushed all to silence as he spoke:
  "My daughter, where is she?
Where are the gifts she sought to lay
  Before her father's knee?
Where, oh ye silent hunters,
  Is the dame so fair to see?"

Then rose the elder brother—
  A counseller to the wise,
And regarding the grey sire, he spoke
  Without a word of guise:
"The fairest of all hunters chose
  To work her own devise.
She left us at the ford, to try
  Her polished weapons keen

On the tired bison we had hurt,
  Behind a woodland screen.
And well we know her aim was good,
  For the pitfall we have seen,
'Twas filled with victory of her art;
  But alas! although we sought
All round the spot, we found her not,
  But a long trail we caught.
A mighty bull had followed her,
  And fiercely with her fought,
For wounds were in his face and neck,
  So bitter had she shot.
And we despatched the bellowing one,
  Where his last wound was got;
We sought her long within the wood,
  And yet we found her not."

Then the grey chieftain answered,
  " To-morrow all shall go
Into the wood with war-gear,
  And beat it to and fro;
And I myself shall lead you,
  For all woodcraft I know."

Well pleased the brethren murmured,
  And then began the feast,
The feast of tired and hungry men,
  The keen meal of the beast;

With ravenous teeth they tore the flesh
  And with swift strokes released
The marrow from the larger bones,
  Or sucked it from the core.
And when the ravenous meal was done,
  When the Cave men, stretched before
The ruddy fires, relaxed their limbs
  And turned them o'er and o'er;
And when the women, placed apart
  And following their lords,
Regaled themselves with daintier bits
  Their wiliness affords;
And ere deep sleep around the fires
  Had banished all discords,—

Lo! running wildly to the camp
  The huntress widow came.
She leaped the limits of the fire,
  Her furs touched not the flame,
And down she fell exhausted,
  The all-victorious dame.

And death was in her cheek and eye,
  The sweet blood, red and warm,
Ran through her breasts; an alien spear
  Had done her mortal harm.
It touched her heart just as she caught
  The fireglow and the charm

Of kindred and of children dear.
  Hard had she been beset,
In the lone forest, by a chief
  That wandering she met.
He strove to take her to his home
  By capture, and beget
Brave sons and daughters by her;
  For well the chieftain knew
No fairer daughter of the Caves
  Than the dame he did pursue,
Or braver with the bow and spear,
  Was known afar, or nigh.
But she disdained him, and she fled,
  Her bow borne up on high,
Eager to find a shelter
  And escape the enemy.

But the wide-breasted chieftain
  Followed her footsteps fast;
And as the glimmer of the fire
  Strook to him as he passed
Her covert, and even as she rose,
  With a last spurt, to meet
The protection of her kinsfolk,
  And rest to wearied feet,
The chief sent forth a hissing spear;
  He did not think to slay—

He only deemed the weapon
    Her fleet feet would delay;
That wounded lightly he would bear
    A new wife safe away.

But she escaped him, and she fell
    Among her kinsfolk dear,
Beyond the camp fire, groaning deep;
    Her heart's blood round the spear,
In throbbing gushes, red and strong,
    Then faint, as death drew near.

They watched her closing gasps of life
    The old chief weeping lay
Beside his fairest daughter,
    And when she passed away
His stiffened limbs were by her
    At the opening of the day.

THE NEOLITHIC FARMER.

THE NEOLITHIC FARMER.

Long before England ruled the waves,
   Long ere the Saxon race
Knew British ports, and long before
   The Celt had found his place
In the forests and the mountains,
   And the vales the streams embrace,
An older folk for centuries
   Uncounted had been here,
And had vanished darkly ere the light
   Of history makes clear
The tale of modern races
   That emerge and disappear
In the written books of authors,—
   These folks had come and gone
When the mystic alphabetic art
   Was utterly unknown.
They have only left their traces
   In mounds of earth and stone,
In graves and mines of limestone
   Where the precious flint was sought,

And cleaved with skill and polished,
　And into weapons wrought.
But of their kin and genesis,
　The whole world knows not aught.

Yet the dark past may rise again
　Before the vision keen,
And our old island's features
　In ancient times be seen,
And this dim farmer-hunter
　May rise upon the scene.

See, from this hill the wide expanse
　Of forest, upland, dale,
Of bleakest moorland and of bog,
　With lake and river vale,
Where the beaver builds his homestead,
　And the wild beasts come at night,
To refresh them after slaughter,
　Or to whet them before fight ;
And starting wild into the woods,
　When the hunter comes in sight.

We look, and see blue wreaths of smoke
　Ascend between the trees,
Thin curling, above tree-tops—
　From human hearths are these ;
We may wander through the forest
　And find the homes with ease.

Green paths are here, the paths of men,
  And while we thread them through,
Beneath the boughs of oak and fir
  The clearing comes in view—
A wide space in the forest depths
  Home-made by capture true;
Won from the wilds by fire and axe.
  And here round huts are raised
In a circle by the hearth fires,
  Where peat and pine-wood blazed;
For the sky is darkening o'er the wold,
  And the fire is warm and kind.
Around are women kneading
  Oaten cakes, and others grind
The corn ears through the hollow quern,
  And matrons spin the wool,
With spindle and with distaff
  Filling the ancient spool.

And not far beyond the homestead,
  Built of stakes and interlaced
With branches of the forest trees,
  A great stockade is placed—
A camp of shelter and defence
  When foes had to be faced;
For here in times of war the herds
  Of cattle and of goat,

Of sheep, of horses, and of hogs,
　By savage dogs were brought,
And the household all assembled,
　And for its treasures fought.

But now the flocks are ranging safe
　Beneath the forest boughs,
Small short-horned oxen, thin-legged sheep
　With straight horns on their brows,
And goats half wild, and hog-maned horse,—
　And swine, lean, gaunt, and small.
The youths and old men watch the herds
　With fierce dogs at their call.
They have spears with polished flint heads,
　And fine ground axes all,
Fixed in their belts of glossy fur
　That bind their bear-skin coats,
And on their feet mocassins gay,
　By hemp-string held in knots ;

And their unkempt locks are mounted
　With caps of beaver skin.
Of stature tall, and sallow-hued,
　And foreheads fair and thin,
With sensual lips, projecting jaws,
　And beardless heavy chin,
Are these, the hunters, and betimes
　First farmers of the soil.

Their wives dig round the homestead,
  And sow with patient toil,
And raise their meagre crops of corn,
  And flax, for dressing fine,
In linen vests, the chiefs and dames,
  And priests when they divine,
And when, with fat anointed,
  They among the people shine
On feasting and rejoicing tides,
  Or at solemn funeral rites,
When some time-honoured warrior
  Falls in the last of fights,
And is placed within his barrow,
  With his war-gear lying near,
The dead hound crouching at his feet,
  As waiting on his spear ;
The dead chief in his gallant robes
  And ornaments most dear.

He gone into the future life
  His soul had seen afar
In dreams and visions of the night
  When all things silent are,
And the soul has revelations,
  No ignorance can bar.

Day closes on the homestead ;
  All the stock is safely led

From the pastures of the forest
  To the fold of the stockade ;
And around the central hearth fire
  Have assembled man and maid,
All the kinsfolk of the commune.
  Old chieftains and their wives,
Their sons and grandsons round them,
  And their brethren, many lives.

And while the great fire rises
  To the softly fanning breeze
That comes with gentle pressure
  Through lanes of forest trees,
Each one finds his taskwork,
  And each one works to please.

Youths polish the hard flint, or fit
  The lance head to the wood,
Or shape the bow, or grease the cord,
  To make it strong and good,
Or grind the stone axe till its edge,
  Frayed, and chipped, and rude,
Grows keen as beaver's cutting tooth.

  And women tend the fire,
And knead and heat the wheaten cakes.
  And old men never tire,

While scraping skins with flint flakes,
  In telling tales of yore,
When they were young and hunted
  The urus and the boar,
The grisly bear and hungry wolf,
  The elk, and many more—
The great game of the hunting field
  That still were roaming free.

But ah ! the old men sighed, " They pay
  No longer hunters' fee,
For our young men are but laggards,
  Wanting strength and subtlety."
Then the youths all jeered in laughter,
  And the maidens caught the jeer,
And archly held up to the chief
  Brave haunches of reindeer,
And hams of bear and bison,
  And the red heart of the steer.

Then they feasted well contented,
  And the old folks went to rest ;
But the young men and their sisters,
  With old lilt and old jest,
Prolonged the night, until the moon,
  Full-orbed, rose high and blest,
And through the forest's glossy leaves
  Its solemn influence shed.

Then all arose and hailed the light,
  And softly bowed the head,
And kissed, with reverential awe,
  Their fingers for the dead.

At last stood forth the homestead's son
  In panoply complete.
His finest tunic he had donned,
  Mocassins graced his feet;
And his head-gear was embellished
  With shells and feathers fair,
And underneath, his hair was moist
  With unctuous fat of bear.
Around his neck a string of teeth—
  Teeth keen and white and rare,
And all of his own capture—
  Hung glittering to his breast.
In finest linen robed; and round
  His skin coat, smoothly dressed,
His ornamented belt enclosed
  A jade axe of the best.

A famous treasure of the tribe,
  It came from Eastern lands,
The birthplace of the race, and passed
  Through many noble hands;
It had been lost and conquered
  From long forgotten bands.

There was Fetish in the weapon—
  A strong protecting power—
In battle, or in enterprise,
  When came the evil hour.
And the possessor held it
  With honour and applause,
But he only bore its virtue
  Upon sufficient cause :
When some high deed had to be done
  Or his kin enforced the laws.

The cheeks of the brave youth are touched
  With bright vermilion dyes ;
Thick lines of red are scored around
  His sloe-black piercing eyes ;
And on his brow blue dotted lines,
  Worked through the skin, comprise
In many graceful windings
  The totem of his race,
A wild swan with its snaky neck
  Arched in unconscious grace,
With its white wings half unfolded,
  As if winging from its place.

The youth addressed the men and maids
  Who jested round the fire.
"You know," he said, "the time must come
  Of a young chief's desire,

When he must win a wife, and bring
  Her home unto his sire
To be a daughter of the tribe.
  My years are now fulfilled;
Wars have I seen, and proved not slow
  When blood had to be spilled;
And in the hunt, I was not last
  When greatest prey was killed.
Nor are my trophies few or vain,
  But such as need not shame
The daughter of a warrior
  And chief of ancient name.
And riches I can add to hers,
  And raise her father's fame."

His brethren heard, his purpose knew,
  And all rose, well prepared
To follow to the homestead
  The lovely maiden shared;
But his blushing sister whispered
  That a few spears should be spared.

She had come into the circle,
  And the ruddy light displayed
Her agile form, in richest dress
  Becomingly arrayed.
Her brother gazed, and smiled, and said,
  " Then trap for trap is laid,"

And a few spears stood behind her.
  Then one brought from his store
A grimly sculptured mantle pin,
  From white tusk of the boar;
Another threw a string of shells
  Her braided tresses o'er.
All with a gift surrounded her;
  And the young chieftain pressed
Upon his heart his sister-twin,
  And tenderly caressed
Her trembling form, and prayed that she
  Might be for ever blessed.

Then issued forth the ruler's son,
  His warriors by his side,
And the thick forest paths pursued
  With a lover's bounding stride;
He knew his safe task was to take
  An unreluctant bride.
His heart was glad, his look was bright;
  His sister in his ear
Had whispered that her capture
  Would be by friendly spear—
The brother of the maiden
  He had chosen for his dear.

High moon above the forest screen
  Shed through its radiant light,

And dappled all the grassy paths
    With pictures dark and bright.
And in the open glades it showed
    The red deer rise in flight,
As they heard the hunter's footfall.
    But the wary brothers passed ;
For though a proud head might have dropped
    Beneath a well-poised cast,
The polished flint was saved until
    A nobler quarry rose,
Whose slaughter would enhance the deed
    Of capture at its close.

Then as they marched they reached the bank
    Of a far winding stream ;
And skirting it, they reached a pool
    Unfathomed, with the beam
Of summer night upon its breast.
    And as they saw its gleam,
The warriors hid and stirred not,
    But waited on the prey—
Some elk, or brawny urus,
    Or brown bear on his way
To meet his matron and her cubs.

And lo ! their luck was good ;
A mighty fur beneath the moon
    Stepped wary from the wood,

And closely passed the covert
  Where the silent brothers stood.

Upon his haunches dropped the bear
  And slily looked abroad;
He passed his fore paw o'er his nose,
  And gently seemed to nod;
But his keen eyes and twitching ears
  His wary nature showed.

The young chief drew his right hand back
  To all its length, and threw
A strong lance; with unerring aim,
  It to the shoulder flew,
And struck beneath it, going deep;
  And then an arrow true
Sank in the neck. And with a roar
  Of rage and mortal pain,
The brown skin rose, and snapped the lance,
  And rushed and reared in vain;
But as his mad eyes saw his foe,
  Up to his feet again
He started, and rushed open-mouthed.
  The chieftain, swift of foot,
Fled, and returned and swiftly smote
  Once more the wounded brute,
And his savage days were ended,
  His savage throat was mute.

The young chief drew his jade axe,
  And drove it through the head.
The brothers with their hunting knives
  The right incisions made,
And tore the thick-furred hide from off
  The white flesh of the dead.

They cached the meat and bore the fur,
  As fitting morning gift
For the daughter of the homestead,
  To whom, with hearts uplift,
They now pressed through the pathway
  With footsteps light and swift.

They reached the clearing in the wood,
  And for a moment stayed ;
They braced their belts and shook their spears,
  And the young bridegroom prayed
And fingered o'er the keen edge
  Of the old axe of jade.

Thrice barking hoarsely like the wolf—
  The totem of the clan
Of the sweet bride—they heard returned
  The notes of the wild swan;
Then through the clearing rushed they,
  And a tumult great began.

The half-tamed dogs gave tongue aloud,
  And all the household woke;
The ready youths had grasped their arms
  Before their fathers spoke,
And the maidens tittered tenderly
  As from the huts they broke.

They threw fresh fuel on the fires
  To show the gay advance
Of the raiders in the clearance,
  And they joined hands in a dance,
While the mimic fight around them,
  With thrust of lance and lance,
And merry badinage went on.
  But the chief was watching keen
For the fleet rush of his maiden—
  She had not yet been seen.

His keen eye saw her passing
  Through the wheat blade high and green
To the forest and the pathway :
  Then his war-whoop sounded high.
His brethren pressed beside him,
  And loud prolonged the cry,
And after the fair damsel
  The loving one did fly,
In the ecstasy of capture ;

But earnest was her flight.
The daughter of a chief must show
　The coyness that is right
And by old usage measured.
　So through the clear moonlight
She fled with speed, nor slackened
　Till her lover, far ahead
Of the other laggard runners,
　Touched her gently with his blade.
She stopped, and fell into his arms,
　And on his bosom laid
Her panting breast, and wept, and cried,
　"Thine am I; I am won.
Thy captive sure, and I with thee
　Till all our work is done
Will live with loved obedience
　To our last setting sun."

With arms entwined, they slowly walked,
　And ere his warriors came
They reached the pool where he had stalked
　And killed the lordly game;
And at its margin waited they,
　Their young souls both aflame.

And soon beside them rest the youths,
　And pleasant homage pay.

And lo! even as the happy group,
  In conversation gay,
Relieve fatigues of conquest,
  They hear, not far away
In the lone forest, gladsome sounds;
  And on the other side
Of the bright moon-lit pool they saw
  Another captive bride—
The sister of the chieftain
  And her captor in his pride,
With his warriors around him.

Then the forest rang around
With loudest shouts of welcome,
  And soon the camping ground
With a brave fire was smoking,
  And the bear's meat was found.
The brides together cooked it,
  And before the feast was done,
With wild music and wild dancing,
  Arose the early sun,
His beams fell through the forest boughs
  And reddened every one.

Stood forth the maiden conquerors,
  And grasped each other's hand,
And the brides embraced each other
  Amid the joyous band.

F

And with many songs and blessings,
  In voices deep and shrill,
They parted by the river-side,
  And the forest fair was still;
The chiefs went to their homesteads,
  Love's ritual to fulfil.

THE EARLY MAN OF AFRICA.

THE EARLY MAN OF AFRICA.

THE Mother-Queen of nations
    Sits shackled on the Nile;
What boots it though a friendly face,
    Wearing a friendly smile,
Has pressed the fetters o'er her hand
    But for a little while?

She is impassive. Ages long
    Have passed since she alone
Reigned mighty mistress of the world
    Upon its oldest throne,
And wielded a wide sceptre
    O'er nations now unknown.
The days of history began
    When her great time had gone.

Greek, Latin conquerors had spoiled
    Her riches, and had drawn
Deep from her soul of wisdom
    Before the Christian dawn.

The Assyrian before them
  Had smote, and left the trace
Of barbarous ruin in his path ;
  But nothing could efface—
Not Macedonia's phalanx,
  Nor the all-subduing pace
Of the Imperial legions—
  The greatness and the grace
Of the Mother-Queen of nations :
  And her immortal dower
Of science, art, and wisdom,
  The thrice-redeeming power
That lifted up the ancient world ;
  Till with a crash it fell,
And the new world half savage rose
  Beyond her mystic spell.
For like her mummies Egypt lay,
  Deep swathed, and hidden well
From the dull eyes of the nations :
  Her wisdom all forgot ;
The clash of swords, the chaunt of monks,
  The shrieks of men who sought
The hell on earth of holiness,
  Drowned every ancient thought.

And when they ceased, the Arab came,
  And for his Allah bore

His bitter sword and torch of fire ;
  And Egypt smote once more.
Trampling her ancient glory,
  Scorning her ancient lore,
The bigots of the Prophet
  Splashed blood on every door,
And subjugated timid souls
  Beneath Islamic sway.
Thus under Turk and Arab heels
  The glorious old land lay,
And lies, although the foot of strength
  Grows feeble with decay.

Sublime it lies, that ancient land,
  Its ruins all around
Of megalithic structure,
  With sacred symbols crowned,
Revealing a long earnest faith,
  Far reaching and profound—
The high peak of the culture
  The human race had won,
In ancient times, the while all tribes
  Of lands beneath the sun,
Were savage and untutored,
  And had not yet begun
To learn the arts of rising life,
  Nor from the Seen to draw

True lessons subtle, simple,
  And worship draped with awe,
Nor to seek in the reflecting soul,
  Philosophy and law.

Egypt, dumb upon the Nile,
  Unknowing and unknown
By the faiths that rose around her,
  Sat on her ruined throne;
The mistress of the secrets
  Of rites were hers alone.
The outward husks were fondled,
  By nations that had grown
In the spell of her enchantments,
  Of her multi-pictured gods;
But they reached not to the mysteries
  Behind the ancient modes,
Nor caught the sacred meaning,
  In the myths the meaning showed;

For from the far-extending past
  This ancient people drew,
By insight and reflecting soul,
  From rude thoughts, thoughts that grew
To wondrous wisdom and forecast
  Of worships, old and new.
Creed secrets of this ancient race
  Still rise before our view;

We know them, and we own them,
    We feel them with the thrill
Of a conscious discovery,
    As if no soul until
Our own had guessed their meaning ;
    And faiths that know no past
Beyond their own foreshadowing,
    In mysteries dim and vast
Out of the superhuman sphere,
    Are high reflections cast
From Egypt's hallowed symbols,—
    The evoluted strain,
Of mighty thoughts, that from the old
    The new had in the grain,
And shape and fashion as it may,
    It ever must retain,
In ever-blooming essence.

    Thus on the flowing Nile,
For ages, with her brooding face
    And tantalising smile,
The Mother-Queen sits lonely,
    And hearing all the while
The hush of the great river,
    And its annual overflow,
That hath never ceased in all the years
    To all the seeds that grow

To yield the fertilising force;
　And blessing men who sow
With certainty of increase.

　Chief goddess it was deemed
Of all the rivers of the earth
　That to the ocean streamed;
And for its sources, noble souls
　Have fought and toiled and dreamed,
And died afar in savage wilds
　Ere yet upon them beamed
The mighty shed of country
　Where the hidden fountain flows—
The secret that for ages long
　Research could not disclose.

But the wide stream has glidden on,
　In flood and in repose,
With procreative splendour,
　And to an empire's seat
Has borne its waves of blessing
　Under Osirian heat,
And bears them to the ruins
　The spoilers made complete.

Whence came this ancient culture?
　From what far distant clime?—

From Ethiopia of the gods,
  When gods were in their prime?
Or from Afric's distant regions,
  Untravelled to our time?

What tribe first issued conquering,
  And after years of strife
Struck its deep roots of empire
  Beside the stream of life?

Who knows?   No sage instructs us,
  No hieroglyphics tell,
Of the first streaks of the glory
  That on the Delta fell,
When to the watered plain there came
  A mighty race to dwell;
And through forgotten centuries
  Of fiercest warfare strove
To keep their fertile strip of soil,
  The blooming field and grove,
From plundering tribes around them,
  Till by their strength they grew
And became the cultured nation
  That the oldest nations knew—
The sources of this primal race
  Lie far beyond our view.

Not forbidden is a vision,
  If the vision may be free,

Of the virgin land's subduers
  In the far antiquity,
If it shapes and bodies out in full
  What earnest dreams may see.

A vision only; let it come
  From an unnumbered age,
And by the Nile's slow-rolling stream,
  Through leagues of swamp and sedge,
In regions where the torrid sun
  Bears down with sweltering rage
Upon the thirsty land; or hides
  Behind a clouded sky
While the warm rain pours ardently
  Until its springs are dry,
And the soaked ground steams slowly
  By the soil's heat on high,

Through weeks and months a steady stream,
  Till the great affluents roar
In swollen floods, and in the Nile
  Abundant volumes pour
Of turbid water, raising high
  The river, till it flows
Majestic o'er its sedgy banks;
  And roused from long repose,
Sweeps swiftly onward all its length,
  And gaining as it goes,

From Abyssinian uplands,
  O'erwhelms, before its close
In earth's mid-sea, by many mouths,
  Egyptian flats of sand,
And in its gradual fall lays down
  Fat on the barren land.

Here in this sun-burnt, rainy clime,
  The swollen river brings
New sustenance to every herb
  That on its drainage springs,
And the reviving rains impart
  Fresh vigour to all things.

The sun breaks from the clouds again,
  And green and golden earth
Smiles in its tropic beauty,
  The beauty of a birth
New from the womb of Nature.
  The grass springs sweet and fresh,
And brings wild herds to pasture
  To repair their famished flesh.

The starred camelopard lifts up
  His long neck from the ground,
His mouth moist with the savoury crop,
  As if he heard around

In his high ears a distant growl
 Or unaccustomed sound.
The hart-beeste, deer, and buffalo,
 Swarm on the verdant sward ;
And the trumpet of the elephant
 In the low swamp is heard,
Long after sundown as he sports ;
 And rising on his guard,
The long snout of the crocodile,
 With evil eyes, is seen
On the edges of the river ;
 His teeth are white and clean,
His appetite is raging,
 And his belly long and lean.

And the huge head of the hippo
 Rises on the river's flow ;
Great mouthed and ponderous of neck,
 He heeds and fears no foe ;
And he wallows, happy in the flood,
 With instincts dull and low.

And the sweet springing of the grass
 Brings other brutes beside,
Following the fattening prey ;
 The lion ranging wide,
And stalking softly on a paw
 That tears the hardest hide ;

He lurks near to the river
  In a covert in the night,
He takes his ease of plunder,
  And shuns the open fight.
Lord of all brutes, like other lords,
  He is lazy in his might,
And only gathers up his strength
  When forced by appetite.

And flesh-devourers follow him,
  Of lesser bulk and power,
But with his stealthy tread of paw
  And skill of place and hour,
With the same pain of hunger
  And instinct to devour
The timorous grass-feeders.

And man too, follows fast,
Upon the sweet-fleshed wanderers,
  And makes his long repast—
After keen toil of hunting,
  With heavy spoil at last—
Upon the fat and tender limbs,
  Cooked by the red firelight,
Beneath a widely branching tree
  Towering into the night,
Where his grass hut of rest is raised,
  His rest of calm delight,
And eager dalliance after chase.

On such a scene we look,
Far in the by-gone ages,
    As we see it in the book
Of some enduring traveller,
    Who yesterday forsook
His home and kindred, high in hope
    That lands unknown before,
By white feet never visited,
    He should visit and explore;
For in these sunny regions
    The change that passes o'er,
In centuries and millenniums,
    The people and their ways
Is as the shadow, for they live
    Lives of the ancient days;
And habits hoar with age survive
    Without a touch of change.
No rudely civilising tread,
    No progress, fast and strange,
Disturb the tribes of Africa,
    In their secluded range.

A broken tribe has gathered
    Beneath the village tree,
To mourn their loss of battle,
    And the friends who could not flee

From the red hour of slaughter
    And the powerful enemy.

O'er-mastered, they had scattered,
    Before a strong assault,
But not before brave warriors
    Had made their final halt,
Some dead in peace, and others bound
    In slave thongs—hapless they !
For never more should they return
    To freedom's blessed day,
To wives and friends and offspring,
    And the headman's easy sway.

Arose up sobs of agony,
    As the chief arranged the clan,
And called out of his memory
    Each warrior, man by man,
And pronounced his blessing on the dead,
    And captives, stricken sore
With hurts from assegai and club ;
    No women to bend o'er
Their wounded miseries, and soothe
    Their pains, and with the lore
Of healing herbs to help them.

But the chief, as it became
A leader of his people,
    And the bearer of a name

G

In other days was known afar,
  With honour and with fame,
Cheered up his remnant warriors,
  And the women by their side,
The wailing wife of captive,
  The widow, and the bride;
With sympathy he cheered them,
  And words of hopeful pride.

No common Afric headman
  Was he; but one of men
Seen rarely among nations,
  One who comes, and not again
Till the times have ripened for him,
  And fit work is for him then.

Of rounded front, and wistful eyes,
  That shone as if they saw
Into the doubtful future,
  Nor could the gaze withdraw,
As though the soul were wrapt away
  In spheres of darkened awe.
Clear olive his complexion,
  And from his great front fell
Thin locks of raven darkness;
  Smooth-cheeked and chinned; the swell
And gentle fall of large fair lips
  Persuasive speech foretell.

Head taller than his warriors,
  And barely past his prime,
He stood before his broken tribe,
  The Prophet of his time,
The Reformer of religion
  In his age and in his clime.

The martyr's struggles he endured,
  Since from his early youth,
Profoundly musing, he proclaimed
  His new faith as the truth,
Of men here, and hereafter ;
  And with the Prophet's sooth,
In fiery words of vengeance
  He doomed the ancient creed
Of Fetishes innumerable
  For every sordid need.
And as he prophesied he knew,
  And counted without heed
Of his own life, the penalties,
  The pains, and bitter war,
His new faith would awaken
  His noble aims to mar.

And hardest fate of all he saw
  His kinsmen move afar,

And with them many warriors
　Who erst beneath his sway
Followed him with loyalty
　As in his father's day ;
But now in firm adhesion,
　To the old ways went they.

High truth consoled him, and the hope
　That truth would yet prevail
Among the dusky tribes of Nile,
　And in its might assail
Their darkened souls and scatter wide
　The errors of the vale.

But the prophet's doom awaited him—
　The doom that since the race
Of human kind made worship
　To thing, or form, or place,
Has befallen every prophet
　Endowed with godly grace,
And who sets his face undaunted
　Against deities debased
And the worship hard and brutal
　That human reason crazed—
The fate of bitter hatred,
　Of priests aroused, amazed.

So found this ancient leader ;
　As his ardent genius rose

With the impulse of true vision,
  More hateful grew his foes,
Till round about his faithful tribe
  Destruction seemed to close.

Despised, rejected, scouted, scorned,
  His teaching fell within
The faithful few, that followed him
  With soul and heart akin ;
They were children of his anguish,
  Soul-born to him and dear,
And nurtured by him gently,
  And now he felt the fear
Of the unsuccessful teacher,
  With evil drawing near ;
For the enemy swarmed round him :
  Then rose he, and with hand
Extended to his followers,
  In jesture to command
Their keen attention, thus he spoke :
  " My people, understand
How we are placed among our foes,
  In this our fatherland.
No hope is there of conquest ;
  We are broken, and before
To-morrow's glowing sun has set,
  If fighting, we implore

Our gods to aid us, we shall be
    A little band no more.

But the gods who watch above us,
    And all our counsels know,
Come to me in their radiance,
    And a hopeful vision show;
And they tell me of a future,
    They can alone bestow.

We must rise and leave our dwelling-place,
    And down the stream of Nile
Pursue, through many days and weeks,
    Our weary way with wile,
So that our hateful enemies
    We may by haste beguile.

A region distant and unknown
    The gods for us hath set;
And we shall find it, though afar—
    No people claim it yet.
And there our huts in peace shall rise,
    And we shall there beget
A nation vanquishing and great;
    And propagating pure
The revelation of our faith,
    That ever must endure;
And the dark children of our foes,
    Our children shall allure

To the high worship they have scorned.
  And empire shall be theirs—
Our children's children—empire vast,
  And with it, empire's cares,
And the large energetic strength
  That plans, and does, and dares.

To this the vision calls us
  By no uncertain call.
Our gods are with us, and they leave
  Our kindred races, all ;
They go with us, and promise us
  Great gain for losses small :

And in the land where we shall rest,
  Still larger sights of truth,
To cherish in our secret souls,
  And show them to our youth ;
Till even darkest mysteries
  Glow with reflected light
From the faces of the Highest Ones,
  Who guard us day and night,
And will with shadowing wings surround
  The progress of our flight.

Clear is the vision in my souL
  My followers, let us rise,
And to the dear protecting gods
  Make early sacrifice ;

Bathe and anoint yourselves, and arm
  For this our great emprise."

The people as they listened felt
  The chief's words fall like rain
Upon the withered meadows,
  Reviving them again ;
Fresh hopes rose up within them,
  And joy succeeded pain.

They saw the vision in his eyes ;
  They caught it in their hearts,
And every bosom burned to seek
  Its glorious counterparts—
Its land of rest and victory,
  Its long enduring days,
And revelations luminous
  To the seer and sage's gaze,
And the wealth of fame and fortune
  No mortal could appraise.

They shouted underneath the tree,
  To mighty gods they swore
That through the hardest toil and strife,
  Afflicted, beaten, sore,
They yet would follow while the chief
  Led onward to explore

The new land of the future,
　With blessings at its shore.

So sunk to rest the people;
　And before the short-lived dawn
Reddened upon the huts, the chief
　Arose, and, Nileward drawn
In anxious contemplation,
　Maintained his great design,
For the vision still before him
　Shone steady and divine;
And he waited for no omen,
　And no other heavenly sign.

As high priest of his people,
　He passed the sacred knife
Across the chosen victim's throat
　And gave the god of life—
Osiris the redeemer,
　The conqueror in strife—
The gushing blood, and burnt the fat
　That clings around the thighs,
A fragrant offering to the god,
　Who bids the sun arise;
And all the people gathered round
　To see the sacrifice.

And then a pillar stone was borne,
　And sunk deep in the soil;

And softly on its top he poured
   The consecrated oil.
To Isis, Mother of the world,
   The sacred stone was reared,
And the high priest proclaimed the spot
   Ever to be revered,
Even as the place where paradise
   Upon the sight appeared.

All fared then to the flowing Nile,
   And drew down from its shore
Their slender boats, and filled them fast
   With women sobbing sore,
And children with their wondering eyes,
   That yet would wonder more
Before the land of rest was won.
   And when the chief and queen
Stepped in their barge of state, and gave
   A signal, that was seen
By all the warriors, every oar
   Dipped in the water's sheen.

With the first movement of the boats,
   The sun through vap'rous haze
Burst in exceeding splendour,
   And shot his level rays,
Till, flooded with the molten light,
   The river was a-blaze.

And every soul was gladdened
  At the omen ; and relieved
The rower dropped his heavy pull,
  And every bosom heaved
A sigh, that swelled into a shout.

The chief's eyes fill with light,
Shining through teardrops, gathered
  During the gloom of night,
And high his solemn voice arose :
  "We do depart in sight
Of Osiris all prevailing."

Then again the oars were plied,
And merrily sang the warriors,
  As down the flowing tide
The light canoes swept onward
  With the river swift and wide.

By sundown many leagues were won,
  And full of hope they drew
Their craft into a wooded creek,
  A grateful rest in view ;
The fires were lit, and supper spread,
  And garrulous all grew.

The first rest on a journey
  Who does not celebrate ?

And though their limbs were weary,
　　Their hearts were full and great;
And far into the solemn night,
　　The husband and his mate,
Young men and maids and children,
　　In joyaunce danced around
The fire-lit trunks of ancient trees,
　　To the entrancing sound
Of their own melodious voices
　　On unfamiliar ground.

Then when the rest was over,
　　And the boats re-stored with meat,
By the huntsmen's skill provided,
　　Rowed on the exploring fleet;
Still onward with the river,
　　With its calms and currents sweet.
So days, and weeks, and months were passed,
　　Nor met they any foe;
The gods had smoothed their journey
　　In the way that they should go.

But the river had its dangers,
　　That were only overborne
By long fatigue and courage
　　And patience, never worn
To impatience and disaster,
　　In the griefs of night and morn.

A waterway had to be cut
  Through miles of fertile weeds,
Netting with bush luxuriance
  From bank to bank the reeds,
And sedges on the flattened shore,
  Where fatal fever breeds.

Nor passed they scatheless through the swamps;
  The children drooped or died;
And shivering mothers passed away;
  And strong men, as they plied
Their cutting tools to clear the path,
  Fell wearily aside,
O'ercome with lethargy and pain.
  And when at last was seen
The unencumbered Nile flow free,
  Through meadows large and green,
With far extending ranges
  Of forests for their screen,
The toilers weened that there at last
  Was reached the fertile land
For which the pilgrimage began.
  And there the pilgrim band
Raised huts, and settled hopefully,
  As if ever to remain.

But the foreseeing chief saw not
  The land they should obtain,

The region that in vision
  Was mapped upon his brain.

But the warriors were weary,
  And the people, travel-tired,
Found in the meads and hunting grounds
  All that their hearts admired—
A land of wealth and fatness,
  And much to be desired.

And there the tribes for years abode,
  Increasing with the years,
Till hoary grew the prophet,
  With age and hopes and fears;
For he knew the gods had ordered
  A home of greater scope
For his people's rising energy,
  And the empire of his hope;
And he dreaded fate unhappy,
  It was ever in his eye—
That when prosperous days were ended
  There would come the battle-cry
Of savages unnumbered,
  In the might of victory.

Yet while peace was on the commune
  His soul, enlarging, sought
To teach his people all he knew,
  Before the world of thought,

Unfleshed and pure, enrobed his soul,
  And dead, he was forgot.

Thus he taught them rules of conduct,
  And laws to them declared,
Of worship to the mighty gods,
  By all the people shared;
And truths of loftier wisdom
  He taught to men prepared
By hidden lessons to receive
  The patriarch's inner light,—
The light that he had gained from dreams,
  And visions of the night,
And lonely contemplations,
  In the forests out of sight.

So passed the years; and lo! at last
  The chief's soothsaying came,
And round the wide encampment broke
  The woe of blood and flame.
Wild Africans surrounded them,
  Of evil name and fame;
And famous battles there were fought,
  Till victory was won
By the people of the prophet,
  The children of the sun.
But many warriors were slain;
  And peace at last was bought

With the exorbitance of cost
  That wakened bitter thought;
And the forewarnings of the chief
  Back to the tribe were brought.

The people clamoured to be led
  Far from the fertile plain,
Where they had flourished mightily
  And purposed to remain—
Where they had raised their altars
  And sanctified their slain,
To the true land of promise;
  The chief rejoicing heard,
And called the tribe to muster
  To hear his latest word;
For a vision was upon him,
  And his aged heart was stirred.

He addressed them:—"Sons and children,
  I am weary, let us go;
And before the gods of silence,
  The Enlighteners, bestow
Their holy seal upon my lips,
  My parting vision know.
This land is not awarded us;
  We must rise and follow far
The windings of the river;
  Its children dear we are.

We must feed out of its bosom,
  We must settle where the shore
Lies green in its caresses,
  And its breadth is studded o'er
With isles of cloudless beauty ;
  There your gods shall evermore
Remain with you and guide you,
  And greatness shall be yours,
And your children following after ;
  All that the soul allures—
The soul, with wisdom girded—
  Your destiny secures.

Fain would I see the landing,
  Fain would I consecrate
Among my havened people,
  By solemn rites of state,
Their first touch on the kingdom
  Their wisdom shall create.

But otherwise the gods decree,
  And ere you reach your home,
Death, and immortal life in death,
  Beyond the arching dome
Of earth, in the untainted sphere,
  Shall call me, as you see
The fulfilment of the promise.
  And if your chief may be

H

Loved and revered, bear to that land—
  His visions eagerly
Revealed with ever growing strength—
  His soulless corpse, and there
Entomb it on a hallowed spot,
  With tribal rites and prayer;
So that still among his people
  He may dead their greatness share,
And await the resurrection
  At the final day of life.
But we tarry, sons and children;
  Let us shun the savage knife,
And once more on the river
  Pursue the end of strife."

His words were as the verdict
  Of the gods supreme and wise;
And the people with approving voice
  And open, glittering eyes,
Bowed all before the prophet,
  And acclaimed, with ardent cries,
The decision of their father;

  Then the village was despoiled
By the women and the children;
  Laboriously they toiled,
In bearing to the river banks
  The treasures of the clan.

And when at length the long canoes
　Were freighted and began
The voyage slowly from the shore,
　A red light fiercely ran
Along the huts and burnt them up ;
　And desolation spread
Over all the grassy meadows,
　And upon the forest shed
A glare of smoke and glory,
　Till in ashes glowing red
The pleasant homes of many years
　Lay in ruin dark and dead.

So on the stream they passed away,
　The chosen folk, to find
The land of promise and of faith
　The seer had in his mind ;
And on the Nile's enlarging stream
　Long days of sunlight 'shined,
And many moons revealed their light
　In crescent form and round,
In fullest splendour and delight,
　Hailed with the happy sound
Of singing voices, while the boats
　Drew lightsomely aground
To rest until the dawning day.
　No enemy they found ;

And the old chief revived, and felt
  As if he should not die
Till the land of his fair visions
  Rose bright upon his eye.
But, alas ! the gods had claimed him,
  And his hallowed end was nigh.

They passed the raging cataracts
  And settled on the stream
Of mighty Nile, withdrawing
  Beneath the potent beam
Of the procreant god's down-pouring
  That swells the soil to team
With a luxuriant promise
  Of harvest.

      But, behold,
They saw their passage blocked with boats,
  And ready to enfold
Their laden fleet, and work it woe.

  Then heaven-inspired, the chief
Rose stately, and commanded
  A pause, observant, brief,
And to the strongest manned, he cried,
  "Strike hard for our relief."

On went the boats, and to the chain,
　That hung from both the banks,
The foremost warriors drove with force
　And clove its battled ranks,
Hurling the spear and striking down
　Wherever showed a face;
And through the wide ensanguined cleft,
　With oars of rapid pace,
The others followed, striking death
　In their victorious race.

And all had passed with little loss,
　And formed again with skill,
For well they knew the enemy,
　Would work them bitter ill
If they should flee before them;
　But they dared to face him still.

Then slowly wheeled the broken fleet,
　And down upon them bore;
A tall, dark chieftain led it on;
　His boat flew swift before
His followers; and as it neared,
　His quick eyes glancing o'er
The brave front of the victors,
　Saw in the barge of state
The aged chief and prophet

Rise valiant and great;
And from his right hand launched he
A spear of evil fate,
For it pierced the vestured bosom
Of the prophet, and he fell,
Death-stricken 'mid his warriors;
Then arose a savage yell,
And a rush as if to victory.

But, behold! an awful spell
Arrested both opposing fleets.
Unsteady from the cast
Of the death-dealing spear, the chief
Swung from his footing fast,
And in the Nile's blue bosom,
He sank, doomed and aghast;

For as he rose and spread his arms,
A monster's jaws upreared
Above the water by his side,
And cruelly they neared,
Till with a sudden snap they tore
His flesh, and disappeared.

The fight was done; the fleets withdrew,
And down the ancient stream
The chosen people bore with grief
Their seer, till evening's beam

Found them a landing, and they laid
    His body, in the gleam
Of bright Egyptian stars, beneath
    A date tree's fertile boughs;
They dressed it, and embalmed it,
    And they swore their sacred vows,
Above the grave in the new land,
    Now found and ever won—
The teeming soil of Egypt—
    Beneath unclouded sun.

THE ARYAN MIGRATION.

THE ARYAN MIGRATION.

THE camp-fires had been lighted,
  Along the river-side,
The horses had been hobbled,
  And the oxen scattered wide,
To feed on the sweet grass and herbs
  The meads and bluffs supplied.

The maids had drawn the udders
  Of the patient, laden kine,
And the men had milked the glossy mares
  With pressure quick and fine,
And had stored the precious liquid—
  Their nectar, most divine.

The evening meal was ready
  Round many smoking fires,
And the wanderers drew thither
  To assuage their sharp desires—
The rising youths and maidens,
  Lords, wives, and great grandsires.

From the upland plains of Asia—
　The great herd-breeding plains,
The homes of their forefathers,
　Where rest their dear remains—
The travellers had wandered
　To realms the Danau drains,

For westward pressed they onward.
　The roving spirit grew,
Even as they marched at easy pace,
　With many a halt in view,
In fertile tracts and clearings,
　In forests, old and new.

Long years before they left the home
　That nursed their roaming race ;
None but the oldest patriarch
　Could recollect the place :
But their home was in their worship
　And their kindred in their face.

Their language and devotions
　The Aryan true revealed,
Foremost of all the tribes of men,
　In wisdom and in build ;
None equalled these bright Easterlings
　In courage on the field.

Unmatched their stately women
  For beauty and for grace,
Clean-limbed and lofty-featured,
  A sweet soul in their face;
It looked out of their hazel eyes,
  And on their brows had place.
They were mothers of great nations
  Still beneath the belt of Time,
Though they wandered unforgotten
  Through many a changing clime;
And history reveals them not
  In primal prose and rhyme.

All had gathered round the camp-fires;
  But before the evening meal
They adore the fires that leap upright,
  And in their flames conceal
The spirit of a mighty god:
  To him they make appeal.

The melted butter on a stone
  They pour, and as the flame
Mounts skyward to the starry night
  Arose the loud acclaim
Of all the wanderers; for the god
  Was by his ancient name

Saluted, and had answered them—
　First in the clouded light,
Then in the pure and smokeless blaze
　That leapt into the night.
And then the evening meal was shared
　By all with great delight;

Rude meal of cakes and flesh and milk
　The people satisfied;
And from old skins the Koumiss
　Was ardently untied—
Drunk deeply by the elders,
　And cautiously supplied
To the middle-aged and younger.
　New joys rise in their hearts,
And vigour to the weary limbs
　The blessèd juice imparts;

And the long, warm day's journey,
　With all its evil fare,
Is forgotten in the pleasure
　Of the vanquisher of care.
The old men's tongues were loosened,
　And their speech was large and fair;
It drew the young men round them;
　And the women, fond to hear,
Sat around the tent doors listening,
　With a smile and with a tear,

For the talk was of the distant home,
    So far away, and dear.

The tale was of their grandsires,
    The grandsons of a Shah,
Renowned for power and riches,
    Enforcement of wise law,
And holy reverence of the gods
    Who rule us all in awe—
(Who from the heaven above us,
    And from the heaven beneath,
Determine all our coming fates,
    And wrap them in a sheathe
Of leaves, from the green Life Trees ;
    Or gloomily enwreathe
Dark fate in leaves of winter
    That on the Death Trees grow) ;
How the young men with their father
    Looked round the land ; and lo !
They knew the gods ordained them
    From the old home to go.

Their father and their kindred
    Filled all the fertile plain,
The valleys, and the mountain slopes—
    A spacious fair domain
And the herds of horse and cattle
    Innumerable, retain

The far-extending pastures.
　But the younger sons had wed—
Already round their tent doors
　Their healthy offspring spread;
The land became too small for them
　Though loved and cherishèd.

"My sons," the wise King counselled,
　"You see we cannot thrive,
Unless the family yields to fate
　Another swarming hive :
For your fast-growing girls and boys
　Will husband and will wive;
Herds they must rear, and feed them—
　And where in all this land ?
But the world is wide for you and yours.
　By the Father-God's command,
You may rise and take your portion
　And keep it by your hand;

And the favour of the gods will go
　Along with you, and cheer
Your marches till you find a home,
　Far, far away, or near
The ancient pastures of our race;
　There you will proudly rear
Great families of kinsfolk
　My eyes shall never see;

But Varuna overlooks us all
 And Indra sheds down free
His glowing procreative heat
 Beneath earth's canopy.
Your cows shall yield their increase,
 Your mares on other soil
Shall suckle healthy foals, and yield
 The sweetener of toil ;
And the stubborn land shall be subdued
 And give you corn and oil.

But remember, oh ! my children,
 The land from whence you sprung,
And the gods your fathers worshipped
 Since the days the race was young.
And teach your children's children
 The hymns that we have sung ;
Make them bow down at the dawning
 When the Usherers of the day
Touch the mountain-tops with beauty,
 Or through the forest stray ;
And teach them meek obeisance
 When the Sun-god bursts away
From the foes that gather round him
 And his glorious car of light ;
Let them pour the holy offering
 At the coming of the night.

I

When the Sky-god wields his thunder
  And disperses arrows bright,
Let them tremble and adore him,
  And amid the Commune raise
An altar to appease him,
  In the old unchanging ways,

At morning ere the day's darg
  Is entered on, upraise
The song of the great Rishis',
  And let all the women sing,
And the children, till to heaven
  The mingled voices wing;
Then shall the song all blessings
  On the long day's labour bring.

And remember, children of my loins,
  To Agni ever pour
The sacred butter clarified—
  To Agni, who of yore
Was the sole god to meet with us
  And dwell at the tent door.

Morning and night remember him,
  For by his grace we thrive,
And round his glowing hearth we feel
  Old energies revive.
He is the father of our race,
  And we could not survive

If he should leave us helpless.
   And let not be forgot
The wisdom of our sages,
   Their lives without a blot;

And keep safe in your memories
   The tales our fathers told
Of our far-roving ancestors,
   And their adventures old
In desert and in forest wild,
   Before there was a fold."

Thus the great father blessed us,
   And bade us forthward find
Our future homesteads in a land
   Befitting to our kind.

"May the All-Father shield you,
   And give to you to bind,"
He cried, "your coming enemies;
   And never may discord
Arise among your people,
   And never may the sword
Be bared, but to avenge a wrong;
   And never may the cord
Be strung upon a bow; or spear
   Be lifted shoulder high,

Except to cover brute or foe
  That lurks your homestead nigh."

And while he blessed us, bitter tears
  Ran down from every eye ;
For all our elder kinsmen
  And their wives lamented sore,
While we, our lot bewailing,
  Drove on our herds before.
Thus we parted from our people,
  Never to see them more.

As the old leader ended
  The sad departing tale,
All round the tents were heard the sobs
  Of hearts that never fail
Of visions of the sunny land
  In lands of snow and hail.

But from his seat uprose a youth,
  The beard just on his chin,
And through his azure eyes the light
  Showed the keen soul within.
He was born upon the weary march,
  In line direct of kin
Of the great chief whose blessings fell
  Upon his own grandsire.

He bent low to the elders,
　And he threw upon the fire
The sacred seeds whose perfume
　The heavenly Ones desire.

And as he rose two beaming eyes
　Forth from the tent door's fold
Regarded him with raptured look
　Through hair of glittering gold,
That overhung a swarthy brow
　And face of noblest mould.

"My father chief," the young man said,
　"The night is not far spent ;
And ere the queenly face divine
　Shines down upon the tent,
Mayhap you will reveal to us
　The toils you underwent
When on your westward journey.
　Great leader of the brave,
You smote the tribes of aliens
　With arrow and with glaive,
And kept your herds in safety
　From wily thief and knave.

Pray tell us of the battles
　You have fought while on the way,
Of the savage men you conquered,
　And the savage beasts of prey ;

For the young men long to hear the deeds
  Done in their grandsires' day."

He ceased ; and in the murmur
  That rose from all around
The hearth-fires and the tent doors,
  A sure accord was found.
The old man looked upon the youth,
  And felt his heart rebound.

" My son," he said, " you task my strength,
  Yet will I not deny
This pleasure to the youths who grow
  Beneath my aged eye ;
And I trust to test their manhood
  Some day before I die.

The fourth moon of our journey
  We parted from the shore
Of the great Caspian waters,
  And dead plains traversed o'er.
Fatiguing was the journey,
  And our cattle suffered sore.

But as the fifth moon showed her edge
  Behind us, we drew near
A forest belt, in whose dark paths
  The pasturage did cheer

Our drooping herds, and yielded us
   Fat limbs of boar and deer.

Through its deep glades we wandered,
   Protected from the heat;
Our herds grew fat and frolicsome
   On the green grass at their feet;
And our young men and maidens,
   Our wives, and children sweet,
Rejoiced in the long arches
   Of woodland in their view,
And sported underneath the boughs
   Of trees that shapely grew.
The days to us were gracious,
   And not a care we knew.

The strong men of us hunted,
   And every night brought home
Fat venison or noble skin,
   Or the red bees' dripping comb,
That thickened sweet on rosy lips,
   Sucking the sweet therefrom.
Nor wanted we adventures;
   For in our hunting raids,
Some monster wild and terrible
   Would start out of the glades;
Nor sped the spears aimed at them,
   Though sharp and biting blades.

Once at a thicket full of thorns,
  Our dogs were baying fierce,
And we, with bow and spear at hand,
  Stood ardently to pierce
The boar when from the thicket
  He rushed with bristling birse;

When lo! a bright-skinned tiger
  Growled, as from out his lair
He sprang, and with his cruel paw
  Struck on my shoulder—there;
He bore me down upon the grass,
  And tore my body bare.

Death hovered in my eyes; and then
  A true, brave brother's spear
Struck through the monster's glossy neck,
  And through the muscles sheer,
Cut to the windpipe, and so fell
  The striped one, lying near
Me, wounded and exhausted.
  But soon my strength renewed,
And home we brought the tiger,
  And by the hearth-fire viewed
His mighty head and cruel jaws,
  And his fierce foot imbued
With blood of mine between the claws.

And then with knife we cut
Through the huge throat and yellow breast,
　　Straight to the open gut;
We tore the bright skin off him.—
　　It now lies in my hut,
And round my old limbs when asleep
　　It wraps me, as the chill
Of winter whitens round the tent,
　　And kindly warms, until
The blessed Ushas drive the night
　　Beyond the western hill.

Thus fared we in the forest;
　　And as our herds were driven
Through its long depths still onward,
　　Under intercepted heaven,
We reached a fertile open
　　The gods to us had given.

Wide it extended, and beyond
　　The eyes' unstinted sight
Were plains of ample verdure,
　　And there we settled right.
We pitched our tents, and fondly hoped
　　For ages to remain
In the great break of the forest-lands,
　　And undulating plain,

With a river wandering through it
  In its journey to the main.
Our herds and flocks grew fast upon
  The green and sweet champagne;

And many years of blissful peace
  In that delightful land
We passed, in hunting shaggy kine,
  And taming to our hand
The brutes as beasts of burden;
  And in digging round the tent,
And sowing strange wild grasses,
  Growing high, and gently bent
In the Autumn red, with golden ears;
  Our fathers' gods had sent,
Unknown to us, our sweetest food.

  But alas! our happy life
Was interrupted in its flush,
  For at last came evil strife:
The wild tribes gathered round us,
  And opposed us knife to knife.
We feared them not. Their fiercest shafts
  Were tipped with splintered stone;
Their spears that sang among us
  Had points of polished bone,
And notched upon the edges
  To hold where they had gone.

Our warriors, with brazen spears
　　And arrows glancing bright,
Killed as they struck with surer aim;
　　And from our bow-strings tight
The fatal shafts on every field
　　Sang out, and won the fight.

But numerous were our savage foes,
　　And when our fights were done
They darkly crept around our camp,
　　And long before the sun
Called us to prayer and sacrifice
　　Much cattle they had won.
They hid them in the desert depths,
　　And slew them one by one,
Feasting for days in plenteous ease;
　　For nothing did they mind
So their imbruted natures
　　Were with flesh and marrow lined.
Thus we suffered, and they bolder grew
　　As we to peace inclined.

Sitting gravely round the camp-fire
　　We, on long debate, agreed
To fold our widespread tents again,
　　And westward still proceed;

The moon should see our rising,
    And our march from off the mead.

Thus our evening fires untended,
    Sunk to ashes white and dead,
And the tents dropped into slumber,
    With many a dreaming bed,
When from the desert round us
    Our dark-skinned foes were led.

They rushed with vigour on us,
    With many a brutal cry;
And though our valiant warriors
    Slept with half-open eye,
The plundering race had won our tents
    Before a spear was nigh.
Straight to my tent their chieftain
    With savage warriors came;
Before I reached my shining arms
    He snatched away my dame.
In his fierce arms he bore her off,
    To my enduring shame.

Soon gathering up my war-gear,
    And shouting loud, I ran
Throughout the Commune, summoning
    Each able, war-clad man;

But woe was me, the force was small,
  For barely could I scan
Four score of spears around me—
  The foe had struck us fell.
But vengeance such as evil gods
  Conceive in Yama's hell
Seized on me, as I ranged my men,
  The while I to them tell
The outrage on my kingly tent,
  And how the savage bore,
Even from my arms, my faithful wife,
  Ere I could stand before
His gruesome presence and defend
  Her sweet form, tightened sore
Around his dusky arms and held
  By his vile fingers tight.

And then I found my kinsmen
  Most eager for the fight;
They swore by Heaven's Father,
  That ere the morning light,
And before the dawn had trembled
  On the hill-tops, they would find
The ravager of homesteads,
  And from his thrall unbind
A mother of the family,
  And give, with bitter mind,

His household to the sword and fire,
　Nor leave his flocks behind.

With hearts ablaze with vengeance,
　Thus fiercely set we out,
And through the lonely desert
　We sped, but oft in doubt
Of the path of the marauders.
　But, as the yellow sprout
Of the horns of heaven's starry queen
　Grew bright upon our path,
The wicked spoor was visible,
　And doubt gave place to wrath.

We urged the fleet feet under us,
　And in a fertile space
We saw the village of our foes,
　And doomed it to disgrace.
The spoilers were before us,
　All was silent round the place;

We halted for a moment,
　Then with the warrior's cry,
We burst upon the village,
　Like red Indra from the sky—
I searching for the chieftain,
　And the hut where he might lie.

Lo ! the village was deserted,
  Not a warrior was near,
Not a woman, nor around the place
  A head of horse or steer ;
They had tricked us in their cunning,
  And in the desert drear,
Had hid themselves and all their spoil.

‘ What fools we are,’ I said,
As around me came my warriors.
  ‘ Back from this bitter raid ;
Let us fall back, and at the dawn
  Strike tents and march, dismayed,
From this dark evil wilderness ;
  For never shall we gain
The princely mother, never take
  Our vengeance for the slain ;
And never find a recompense
  Long as we may remain
For our horses and our cattle.’

And they reluctant turned,
And onward through the desert,
  Our swelling bosoms burned.
Glad were we once again to find
  Our tents not overturned,
And all our families in peace.

So when the new light broke
We brought our herds together,
　And gave warning to our folk,
And ere the glorious god had shown,
　We mustered every flock,
And in marching gear were ready,
　Seeking still to be enhomed.
But far though we have sought the boon
　And far though we have roamed,
Has no dear spot been found for us.
　We are Aryans marching on,
To the wild west yet before us,
　Flesh of flesh and bone of bone,
All brethren seeking rest and ease,
　And they shall come anon ;
For the father's blessing stays with us,
　And the gods our fathers bent
With reverence and awe before
　Still watch around our tent.

Thus with warrior hearts we started
　That bitter morning, rent
By cries of wives and daughters,
　Despairing cries of woe,
For the fair mother of the tribe
　Was captive of the foe,

And my own eyes were filling full
From a sad heart's overflow."

He ceased, the old man, and retired;
And the silence of the night
Was broken softly by the voice
Of the brave youth of might,
The future leader of the tribe,
And master of the fight
When war is born of plunder.
And with his voice he rose,
And bent unto the elders,
While the ruddy fires disclose
The reddening flush upon his face,
And all his fair hair glows
In gleams of the red metal:

"Must we still westward go,
Are we still forced to wander
While toils upon us grow?
Our family is growing great—
Its increase who may know?
Or may we not on these great plains,
Through which this mighty stream
Of azure water slowly wends,
Secure the patriarch's dream—
A happy home to feed our herds—
And end our wandering ways?

K

Here may our aged grandsires
   Fulfil their later days;
Here may young men and maidens
   Their tents of love upraise."

And as he spoke sweet laughter
   Rippled around the fire.
"Nay," said he, lowering his eye,
   "'Tis not the sole desire
Of those who wish to leave the tent
   To light their own hearth-fire;
Though such should be an Aryan's wish,
   What time his soul has skill,
To lead away a maiden,
   Subdued unto his will,
And rear an Aryan family
   And the high law fulfil.

I speak for a decision,
   And let the wise decide:
Here, will I stay, or I will go,
   And take with me my bride.
These lands are rich and spacious:
   Shall we wander, or abide?"

The youth sat down, and murmuring
   Around the camp fires swelled,

For as he spoke, there gathered
  All the encampment held ;
And against his eager argument,
  No youthful heart rebelled.

But as the murmurs died away
  Arose the Sire of Song.
The gifted and far-seeing,
  He in his memory long
Had all traditions of the race ;
  And in the right and wrong
Of quarrels and of questions
  That vexed the Commune's heart,
His words were healing, solving,
  For the wise gods took his part.
And all the brethren looked to him,
  In the trouble and the smart
Of evil days and sad defeats.
  He prophesied and sang
All along their many wanderings ;
  And his songs at gloaming rang
Round the fires, when they were kindled,
  And at dawning when the clang
Of milking-pails was heard around.

  An old man, nearing now
Upon his fourthscore birthday,
  Bald and furrowed on the brow ;

But his blue eyes had the fading light
  Of that far-western shore,
Where twilight reigns, when death has come.
  Where man is man no more,
And the dull silent life prevails
  Of shadows flitting o'er
A dream of fields and forests.—

He arose, and raising high
His hand above the beaming youth,
  Experienced did reply.
" My son, you question fit and fair ;
  Your purport I descry.
There are aged men amongst us,
  There are fathers growing old,
Many young men and maidens
  Are here within our fold ;
And we have reached these grassy plains—
  May we not rest in peace,
And keep the land by spear and sword,
  The while our herds increase ?

But the gods have bade us wander,
  And not yet may we cease.
The fate is on our children ;
  But here the old may rest ;

And as the father patriarch
  Sent our fathers, rich and blessed,
Forth from the ancient pastures,
  So may we, heart oppressed,
Send you, our kindred, onward,
  And with your chosen wives,
And your share of kine and horses
  To begin your separate lives,
Still westward, till another land
  With streams and pasture drives,
Even such as these, delight you;
  There you may prosper well,
And perhaps before your fathers
  In the silent meadows dwell,
You may to children's children
  A departing tale foretell."

He ceased; and all the young folks heard
  His words divinely weighed;
And though many souls were gladdened,
  There were others much dismayed,
For the love of kindred bound them
  And a sweeter feeling swayed.

To them the fair-haired Prince a word
  Of counsel uttered then:

"We are no longer children
    We are grown-up, bearded men ;
It befits us to obey the sooth
    Within the prophet's ken.
What fear we ?   As our fathers passed
    Through dangers, so shall we,
And as they struck, so we shall strike
    Whatever foe may be
In hated ambush on our path
    Or in the open free.

And since the gods decree our course,
    What Aryan shall refrain,
From resolute obedience,
    If in his soul remain
A spark of the ancestral light
    That guides through shaw and plain ?

Up, then, my brothers, and prepare,
    Choose ye your loving mates,
For ere the sky has three times ope'd
    Her golden burning gates,
To the bright steeds of Indra
    Our march shall have begun.
And I your leader, if so be
    You choose me, who have won,
Though young, the praise of elders,
    Will lead you with the sun."

Then even timorous souls grew large,
　And round the fires applause
Rose to the constellations—
　A chief espoused their cause,
And as their head would lead them
　In the wisdom of their laws,
In the might of their old heroes.

And so the tents were closed,
The fires before them dwindled,
　And the kinsfolk all reposed.
But, before he laid him down, the youth
　Glanced round ; and half disclosed
By flickering fire-light, saw his love.
　And she who sought his eye
Rushed eager to his side, and clove
　To him with maiden cry.

Then softly walked they from the tent,
　To the Danau, rolling nigh ;
There by the slowly winding stream
　Their love vows were renewed.
She had heard unseen the high debate,
　And in her heart subdued
All other feelings for her love ;
　And he who gently sued

Her wifely presence with him
　　In the far, untrodden lands,
Found in her dear love clinging
　　And fervid grasp of hands,
The rain his soul had thirsted for,
　　To quench its burning sands.

And, as they talked, new life to both
　　Was opening in the wild ;
No longer seemed the parting day
　　A day to be exiled,
But rather the sweet birth of love
　　That parting reconciled—
He high in life ; she confident,
　　As in his face she smiled.

The parting morning came ; and all
　　The kinsfolk, roused from sleep,
Assembled round the father's tent,
　　The ancient forms to keep,
In reverent simplicity,
　　And sorrow, true and deep,

As from the family's bosom
　　The loved ones march away.
The sacred rites were soon performed,
　　And in their best array,

With wives and herds, with spear and shield,
  In the faint dawn of day,
The youthful band of Aryans
  Moved slowly from their kin,
And westward took their journey,
  New lands and homes to win.

THE BURNING OF THE CRANNOG.

THE BURNING OF THE CRANNOG.

THE morning breaks upon the lake,
  And through the shivering leaves
Of the wild woodland, early light
  Its placid breast receives.
It glinted on an island home,
  And lighted up the eaves

In sheltered corner of the mere.
  The isle was founded deep
On piles and crossbeams deftly stacked
  And morticed, till the heap
In rounded form arose above
  The water; and around
A high stockade was firmly fixed.
  On the half-floating ground,

In its centre rose the homestead,
  Built up of birchen logs,
And thatched with ferns and rushes
  From the woodland and the bogs;

With cattle-sheds beside it,
  A homestead all complete.
And surrounded by the water,
  Safe it seemed to be, and meet
To cope with any enemy,
  Though strong of arm and fleet;

For though a gangway fixed on piles
  Reached to the nearest shore,
Down in the lake it was concealed
  Sufficient, and no more,
To let the cattle wade to land,
  And home when day was o'er.

A tree boat, hollowed out by fire
  And bronze axe, floated near,
The paddles lying in its stern
  To quickly oar and steer;
It was the ready messenger
  Of the farmer of the mere.

Day broke; and summer warmth awoke
  The homestead folk to thrift;
The old man, grey and bowed, to watch
  His cattle, turned adrift
To find their pasture in the woods;
  But first he did uplift
His old hands to the sun and prayed,
  The while the glittering rays

Shone on his furrowed face, and set
  His white hair in a blaze.
That peace would be his children's lot,
  And many prosperous days.

His strong sons sallied out and cast
  A reverent glance on high,
Then blithely to the cattle-sheds
  They, with a sister nigh—
A dark girl, light of foot, and shaped
  With wondrous symmetry—

Passed on; she bearing in her arms
  Her milk-bowls, to be filled
With white juice from the udders,
  That at her pressure rilled
And foamed within the earthen bowls;
  And the morning milking done,
The kine and sheep were driven forth.
  Slow, blinking in the sun,
They marched through the rude gateway,
  And the well-known gangway won;

And small limbed swine and horses,
  With shaggy coats, went out,
And made for the green forest,
  With many a warning shout

From the brothers, who with spear in hand
  The struggling herds controlled,
And drove them all in safety
  To the pastures of the wold.
They landed lightly on the grass,
  And to the homestead old,
They waved their arms and disappeared
  Within the forest glade;

And father, mother, sister smiled.
  And he the aged said,
For a fateful look was in his eye
  As of a coming raid,
" May no foul enemy be near,
  No red-haired, blue-eyed foe,
To steal our cattle, smite our sons,
  With iron in the blow."

Mother and daughter proudly smiled;
  The men were strong of limb,
In war-gear clad, with spear and knife,
  Hard fighting, fierce and grim,
When rage of battle seized them,
  And the eye of fear was dim.

In hunter's skill and forest lore,
  No better men could be;

They knew the wild boar's lair, and where
  The wolf made quarters free;
They smote the red deer in the glades,
  And on the far off height
They tracked the reindeer by his spoor,
  And smote him in their might.
And wild bulls, roaming in the fields,
  Still fiercer in the fight,
They conquered with the edge of bronze,
  Nor turned they from the fray,
By plundering tribes provoked, but stood
  Through many a bloody day,
And never yet had met defeat,
  Or the fell wounds that slay.

The sun shone down upon the lake
  In prime of summer heat,
As from the stockade passed the girl,
  And forthwith took her seat
In the tree boat that floated near;
  And handling firm and neat
Her double-bladed oar, she made
  The light boat skim along,
Beguiling the fair voyage
  With snatches of a song—
Old song of love and cruelty,
  Of victory and wrong.

L

And fair and trig the maiden looked,
  Her steady large brown eyes
Shone eager from her face, and showed
  A soul without disguise.
Her glossy hair of darkest tint
  Was coiled in braided ties,
And rose above her earringed ears ;
  And round her neck was strung
Of vitreous beads a triple row,
  That rainbow colours flung.
Her fur-trimmed mantle at her breast
  Was fastened by a dart,
Of red wrought bronze, a token
  From one who felt the smart
Of love within his bosom,
  And showed it by his art,
And in her girdle was a knife,
  Keen edged of ruddy hue,
And in her boat beside her lay
  A spear with handle new.

She reached the shore, and beached her boat,
  And, spear in hand, she passed,
With buskined feet into the wood,
  And round about her cast
To find the fresh prints of the herds ;
  And ranging long, at last

She found them in a shallow glen ;
　Through which a streamlet flowed ;
There the sweet grass and brackens grew,
　And there. the wild flowers blowed.
And when she called the cattle came,
　And softly to her lowed.

She drove them to an open glade ;
　And as they grazed around,
The fearless girl, with spear in hand,
　Surveyed the neighbouring ground.
And while she walked, she heard the rush
　An old familiar sound,
Among the brushwood of the boar ;
　Then stood she, lance in hand,
Poised for a stroke if he should come,
　And nobly did she stand.
Eyes eager, and unflinching nerves
　In mouth, and hand, and foot,
Showed how she would encounter
　The white-tusked, brawny brute.

He came with feebly snorting snout,
　His strength struck at the root,
A spear had pierced him to the heart,
　And from his side gushed red,
In spasms, his unholy blood,
　And near her he lay dead.

And after him a warrior came,
　The hunter who had led
The long pursuit, and gave the wound
　From which the tusker bled.

He stood, a youth with auburn hair,
　Beside the eager maid;
The boar was at her feet, and she
　Upon his side had laid
Her brazen spear, but not to claim
　The quarry; for she said,
"Thine is the conquest, mighty chief;
　He fell beside me here,
The death-blow given by thine arm
　And thy unvanquished spear.
So take him : he is thine; for we
　The forest laws revere."

But the brave youth made answer,
　"Nay, maiden; I shall draw
The boar down to the water-edge,
　For thine he is by law,
If not of forest, yet of love—
　Sweet daughter of the lake.
For thee I haunt the forest depths,
　And only for thy sake;

My people are not thine, but them
  I gladly would forsake
To live with thee and with thy folk,
  And ever severed be
From all my kindred if I might
  But live in love with thee.
Sweet meetings we have had—and I?—
  Am I not dear to thee
As thou to me? Alas ! our race
  For ever is at war
With thy brave people ; ours has come
  By conquest from afar,
And must prevail, for strength is ours
  And Fate's ascending star."

Then as he ceased he clasped her round,
  And down upon the grass
They sat and talked, nor noted they
  How shortened hours may pass,
Until the kine, with udders swelled,
  From deep chests bellowed near.
Then rose she, blushing, half in love
  And half in guilty fear.
"Now I must go," she said, "and drive
  My herds down to the mere—
The patient herds; for see you not
  The sun draws to the sea,

And soon my brethren will return ;
  Spoil laden may they be."

" Nay, maiden, I will speed thy way,"
  He said, and hastily
Swept round the herds and drove them on ;
  Then on his shoulders wide,
He threw the tusker he had killed,
  And strode on by her side ;
And through the woodland passed they
  Like warrior groom and bride.

They reached the brook that tapped the lake,
  When bitter battle-cries
Aroused and stopped them, and each looked
  Into the other's eyes.
" My brothers ! " cried the maiden ;
  " My kinsmen ! " cried the chief ;
The boar fell from his shoulders
  And he struck his hands in grief.
She raised her spear, and vehemently
  Rushed forth to their relief.

" Stay ! " cried he ; "drive the cattle home—
  The lake is near at hand ;
And I will stop the battle,
  Though I fight my own brave band,

If warriors have not fallen
 And blood be on no brand."

"Haste, then," she said, "and I will wait
 With boat upon the strand."
And as she spoke he disappeared,
 And she with spear in hand
Drove down the eager cattle
 To the lake, and saw them land.

She drew the boat upon the mere,
 And softly stepped within,
And sat with oar and spear in hand,
 Her nervous nostrils thin
And eyes dilated, as if she
 Felt battle through the skin.
Nor long she waited ; brethren three
 Ran gasping to the boat,
With bloody weapons, and with blood,
 In many a purple clot,
Upon their faces and their arms—
 The battle had been hot.

Some quick strokes of the paddle took
 The boat beyond pursuit
And her face turned to her brothers
 As a soul with terror mute,

And her eager looks were questions.
  They sorrowful replied,
"Three of us in the forest lie,
  With foemen's blood bedyed,
And we too should have fallen
  In the battle by their side—
For foes pressed hard upon us,
  And outnumbered us by far—
Had not a chief ran in between
  And claimed an end of war,
And bade us haste to meet thee
  While he pursuit could bar."

But gleams of vengeance passed across
  Their faces as they told
Of the great deeds of their brothers
  Ere their hearts were stricken cold;
For each his stalwart man had slain,
  And one whose weapon old
Twice cut a life before it fell
  Out of his nerveless hold.
And they too had repaid the blood
  Drawn by the bitter sword,
By harder blows and fuller streams
  That gashes wide afford;
But hopeless was the contest
  Against the stranger horde.

"What then," the maiden said, "is come
  At last our hapless doom;
Must we all perish innocent,
  To give the new race room?
The land is wide, and we might live
  Together without hate;
But their insatiate appetite
  No conquest can abate.
And none but they must share the land
  Our fathers strong and great
Won from the wild beasts of the field,
  The forest, and the hill.
And you have slain their braves, and struck
  Blows that do all but kill.
Oh! do believe, my brethren dear,
  They purpose further ill;

Their cry for vengeance will not fail—--
  Not even counsels fair,
Such as the noble chief will give,
  Their purpose will defer.
They will attack our island home,
  And slay us in their snare.

But we may fly and leave the lake
  For life to all is sweet;

Thus the old sire and mother dear
  Their days may fill complete;
And we some other home may find,
  Where foes we shall not meet."

Her pleading words fell on the ears
  Of men of courage true.
They knew fate was against them,
  That the bravest man who drew
His sword against a hundred
  Would fall before a few.
Their lake-girt home was past defence
  If the strong alien band
Its capture or destruction
  Should of the chief demand.
The night fell softly as they moored
  The boat upon the strand.

Then passed they to the hearth-fire,
  And beside its flickering light
They solemnly assembled,
  These young men red from fight;
And their sister told the story
  Of death-sorrow and of flight.

The bitter meal was over,
  They were all prepared to fly,

When burning arrows lighted up
  The darkened lake and sky. .
They lighted on the roof-tree,
  And the flames ascended high,
And others followed fast, and showed
  From whence their flight arose.
Their foes were on the lake, and manned
  The waters to enclose
The crannog-dwellers and their home,
  Their cattle and their gear ;
And nought remained but death by fire,
  Or fierce point of the spear.

Then the heroic maiden spoke,
  "Save you our parents dear,
Secure the boat, while from the sheds
  The cattle I unbind,
And drive them down in mad stampede
  Into the lake behind.
Follow them not, but watch our foes,
  And if the gods are kind,
The herd may tempt them to pursuit,
  And we may steal ashore,
And seek a place of shelter
  Till the dread night is o'er ;
For back into our homestead
  We shall return no more."

Without reply she ran within
  The red illumined sheds,
Released the brutes, and out they burst,
  And rushed with lowered heads
At the stockade, and forced their way
  Into the waters deep ;
And terror-stricken horses
  Made many a fatal leap,
And followed through the gaps, the flock
  Of singed and trembling sheep.

Now stole she back to reach the boat ;
  She saw it by the light
Of her own burning home, the scene
  Of an unequal fight,
For the aliens' spears surrounded it ;
  It sunk into the night.

Alone upon the burning isle,
  The maiden nerved her heart
For a short contest and the stroke
  From arrow or from dart ;
Then to her loving kindred,
  Dead, she would, dead, depart.

The fight was over, but the flames
  Spread fast upon the isle ;

The crannog of her fathers
  Might be her funeral pile.
But the water lay around her,
  Her foes she might beguile.
She could pace the hidden gangway,
  Or if danger should be there,
She would swim and reach the woodland,
  And if once beneath the care
Of the ghosts that haunt its shadows,
  She was safe from evil fare.

But as the firm resolve had come
  To strike out for the shore,
She heard the paddling of a boat,
  And she trembled to the core,
Till a low sweet voice assured her.
  He had come, the battle o'er,
To succour her in danger.
  He had sought her in the strife,
The dire strife of her kindred,
  Short and noble; life for life,
They fell avenged upon his men
  Opposing knife to knife.

Then in the boat he placed her,
  And ere, the woodland's marge
He oared her to; they sat and watched
  The smoke and flame enlarge,

Till they covered all the island.
   And the homestead ever dear
Burnt down unto the water's edge
   Did ever disappear;
And the dark silence of the night
   Closed round about the mere.

THE LAST SACRIFICE.

THE LAST SACRIFICE.

[The scene of this, the last of the Sagas, is laid at the site of
a cromlech well known to archæologists, and named the "Auld
Wives' Lifts," on Craigmaddie Moor, in Stirlingshire, N.B.
As described in the Saga, the cromlech is in the centre of
a natural hollow, and is formed of three large stones, two upright and one across the top, a large stone, weighing between
twenty and thirty tons. The upright stones taper from the
bottom, so that between the "coping stone" and the uprights
there is a space, through which one person may with some little
difficulty pass. It is still a superstition in the district that the
engaged pair who pass through and return will find good
luck to follow them in their married lives. The origin of the
name "The Auld Wives' Lifts" is unknown, though there are
numerous fanciful legends of an explanatory nature that have
been worked into local story and song. Within a mile or two
of the cromlech, the great battle of Mucotoc—modern Mugdock—
was fought in the seventh century, and, as described by Nennius,
must have been of a decisive character, as between different
races of Celts. The curious reader will find Professor Rhys'
explanation of the battle in his admirable little book on "Celtic
Britain." Though not above ten miles from the great western
metropolis of Scotland, the district is to the present day a lonely
one, and its inhabitants still retain many old customs, and hold
to many old prejudices. Mugdock, it may be stated, is now only
known in Scotland from its great reservoir, constructed by the
Corporation of Glasgow for the purpose of storing the water
supply from Loch Katrine—a supply which accommodates about
a million of people.]

M

Upon a dark and rainy night
  I struck across the moor
With hurried steps, and stayed not till
  Upon its topmost floor
Of velvet grass—a fairy ring—
  A place I knew of yore,
I stopt to breathe, to strike a light
  And kindle a cigar.

And there in patience I remained ;
  For in the clouded lift
Slight streaks of brightness slowly broke
  Into an azure rift,
And from th' engulphing clouds the moon
  Drove to it round and sweet,
And on the dreariness of moor
  That lay around my feet
Shone with a clear and gladsome gleam ;
  It lighted far below
From where I paused a hollow ring,
  Where treacherous marshes grow,

And in the hollow's centre high
  An ancient altar shone—
Two upright rocks, and on the top
  A massive round of stone.
Beneath the uprights one could pass
  Beneath the coping block ;

And country people yet will bow
  Beneath the sacred rock,
For luck attends the youthful pair
  Who pass and do not mock.

Dreams drew me to it, as above
  The night was clearing fast,
And down into the marshy ring
  With wary feet I passed;
And soon upon the altar stone
  I clomb; but first went through,
For luck and ancient custom's sake,
  The sacred avenue.

I stood upon the ancient pile
  And looked up to the sky,
Watching the water-laden clouds
  In masses, drifting by,
The moon absorbed, then bursting forth
  In rounded radiance bright,
And for a brief space making day
  Of the uncertain night.

And, glancing round, it seemed to me
  A crowd came into sight,—
Of men and women, boys and girls.
  In ordered march they came

Over the moor, and as they neared,
  I thought I knew their aim—
Some sacred deed they meant to do,
  Some rite of ancient name.

Then down a low edge of the ring
  They silently deployed;
While watching from the vantage ground
  The cromlech's height supplied,
And under fitful gleams of light,
  Their forms I well descried.

Not of the living time were they:
  A dead race seemed to rise
From the eternal past—the past
  Unknown to histories,
Or only darkly known to those
  Who ancient mounds explore,
And find forgotten ancestors,
  Forgotten—and no more.

And here they came in scanty robes,
  A small race, pale of skin,
With dark hued hair, and tattooed breast
  To savages akin;
And in their midst, a stately form,
  That might be priest or king.

He ranged them with a leader's skill
  Within the sacred ring,
And raised aloft upon the night
  A song for them to sing.

And by the princely chief, sustained
  By maiden arms, I saw
A tall-grown girl, in bridal white,
  And looked upon with awe
By elders of the tribe, for she
  Seemed doomed by a dread law.
A fair face patiently composed,
  And limbs of lithely grace,
Thick tresses on her shoulders fell
  And wantoned on her face—
A fair face, lit with vivid eyes,
  That glanced around the place.

The crowd had reached the holy spot,
  And circling round it spread,
The noble leader took the maid
  By the right hand, and led
Her to the hollow pass, and thus
  Addressing her, he said :
"Go through, my daughter, and again
  Come backward, and once more
Pass and repass, while all the folks
  Your faithfulness adore."

She gathered up her robes, and passed
   Beneath the altar stone,
And underneath I heard her foot
   Slip softly, as alone
She glided through and through, and wrought
   The spell without a moan.

Then upward to the sky the priest
   Stretched out his hand and cried,
"Protect us, O ye mighty Ones,
   And be ye satisfied;
A princely maid we offer ye;
   She cannot be denied."

From out his belt a whetted knife
   He took, and placed it bare
With reverent hand upon the stone.
   Its savage glitter there
Appalled me; at my foot it lay
   With unremitting glare
In the clear moonlight; for it seemed
   That I should stand and see
The white breast of the maiden cut,
   And her warm blood flow free,
To satiate the awful rage
   Of a barbarous deity.

The priest laid down the knife, and took
  The damsel in his arms;
He kissed her softly on the cheek,
  Gazed chastely on her charms;
And while the tears ran down his face,
  He on the altar raised
Her trembling body, and anon
  Turned to her folk, and praised
The willing sacrifice of youth,
  And cried, "Be not amazed
That the great gods of heaven and earth
  Should seek a victim rare,
The tenderest bud of innocence,
  High-born and chaste and fair;
The noblest damsel of the tribe,
  The holy virgin there."

He ceased, and at a signal came
  Two aged chieftains near;
They bound the virgin's hands and feet,
  With many a sigh and tear;
But never from her white lips came
  A sound that I could hear.

The priest climbed on the altar,
  And decently composed

The fair form of the noble girl;
　　Then in his hand enclosed
The dreadful sacrificial knife,
　　And raising it on high,
To the full moon and stars divine,
　　That glistened in the sky,
He called the people round him,
　　And the people made reply :

"Oh, men of vales and grassy hills,
　　We are encompassed round
With many foes; but here we meet
　　Upon this sacred ground ;
And by the holy altar, raised
　　By forefathers renowned.
This place, the ancient chosen spot
　　Where the divine ones rest,
And listen with a willing ear
　　To every request
That shapes itself within the tribe,
　　And grows within its breast.

Last of our country's faith are we,
　　And if I may divine
From pregnant sayings and forecasts
　　Of Seers of noblest line,
This maiden sacrifice shall be
　　An awful final sign.

If her pure blood flows fast upon
  This altar, so shall we
Shed blood, and be the conquerors
  Between the sea and sea,
And our true faith in triumph win
  Its ancient mastery."

Then stood he by the virgin's side—
  He almost touched my feet—
He shook, and sobbed, and cried in pain,
  "My daughter, pure and sweet,
Thy mother's likeness and her life,
  My soul white and complete,
Forgive thy father-priest, and say
  You know what now we do
Is for the favour of the gods,
  And their protection true,
And to avert our people's doom
  From creeds and races new.

A moment's pain—thy self shall pass
  To unexampled bliss,
And thy dear mother in her arms,
  With many a tender kiss,
Shall welcome thee, and shield thee
  From a dark time like this.

And shed soft tears of love for him
  Who strikes the sacred blow,

Who feels as if thy blood were his,
  As if the stroke should go
Straight to his heart, and not to thine,
  That the red flood should flow
Upon the altar from his veins;
  For, loved one, he would fain
The gods would take his life for thine,
  And let thee here remain
To wed a foeman, though he be
  Chief of the alien race.
But the gods who nursed us long ago,
  And gave us strength and grace,
Who gave us herds and hunting-ground
  In this green valley's space,
Forbid it; and they claim thy life
  A precious sacrifice.
But when the dreadful rite is done,
  Death also in his eyes,
Shall after happy battle
  Victorious arise;

Yea, daughter, he shall come to thee,
  And to thy mother dear,
His vexed and anxious soul released
  By hard thrust of a spear;
And, mounting upwards, claim you both,
  In the unblemished sphere.

The gods so will it, for he knows
　　The fateful hour is near."

Then grasping with impassioned force
　　The virgin, standing tall
Upon the altar, he upraised
　　Her fair form, and o'er all
Her white face pressed his kisses,
　　And gently let her fall.
She murmured softly in his ear,
　　" So be it, at Their call."

Stood up the priest to all his height,
　　And to the people turned;
" You know," he said, " how keen my soul
　　Has for this maiden yearned,
And that some other sacrifice
　　The gods would not have spurned,
I prayed to substitute; but Fate
　　Is all, and over-lord,
And even the high gods must take ·
　　Its unrelenting word.
The doom must fall upon this breast,
　　The pure and the adored."

Then raising higher still his voice
　　In rugged tones and true,

"Sing out," he cried, "ye people,
　　The song for ever new,
Though old as our religion,
　　That to the rite is due."

The people paused a moment,
　　And then their voices rose,
Slow, solemn, like the music
　　That through the valley flows
In summer midnights, when the shades
　　Do battle with their foes:

———

"God of the Light, to thee
　　Our deepest yearnings go.
Thou bringest us the Day,
　　And work and bliss and woe.
Thine eyes shine on us ever,
　　From dawning unto night;
And strong in thee we hunt,
　　And strong in thee we fight.

And thou, the god of blood,
　　Who askest the sacrifice,
Strongest of all the gods,
　　The strong one, and the wise,
On thy high altar here,
　　And in the sacred sight

Of the eternal vault
    And its mysterious light,

We raise the song to thee,
    And pray thee to be here,
While on the blessed stone
    Is laid the victim dear.
The untouched blood of youth,
    Accept, and as it flows
Redeem us, and protect us,
    Oh, God, of war and woes !"

Lo ! as the song sunk on the night,
    Arose victorious cries,
And fast adown within the ring
    A band of warriors hies,
And scatters with the sword the crowd
    That waits on sacrifice.

Upon the altar leapt the chief,
    And set the maiden free,
And but for his protecting arm
    The rite of cruelty
Had been accomplished, and the knife
    Had sped the prophecy.

But bravely died the priest ; the blade,
    Hallowed by many a rite

Of sacrificial virtue gleamed
  The last time on the night—
It struck into his noble heart,
  Deep buried out of sight.

Prone on the sacred stone he sank,
  His dark blood rippled o'er
Its rugged surface, dabbling red
  Behind me and before.
An awful victim, and the last,
  He fell ; and rose no more
The race he led, the faith he held,
  The gods he did adore.

THE END.

PRINTED BY WILLIAM CLOWES AND SONS, LIMITED,
LONDON AND BECCLES.

CHATTO & WINDUS'S
LIST OF BOOKS.

✿ * * * * * ✿ * * * * * *

About.—The Fellah: An Egyptian Novel. By EDMOND ABOUT. Translated by Sir RANDAL ROBERTS. Post 8vo, illustrated boards, **2s.**; cloth limp, **2s. 6d.**

Adams (W. Davenport), Works by:

A **Dictionary of the Drama.** Being a comprehensive Guide to the Plays, Playwrights, Players. and Playhouses of the United Kingdom and America, from the Earliest to the Present Times. Crown 8vo, halfbound, **12s. 6d.** [*In preparation.*]

Latter-Day Lyrics. Edited by W. DAVENPORT ADAMS. Post 8vo, cloth limp, **2s. 6d.**

Quips and Quiddities. Selected by W. DAVENPORT ADAMS. Post 8vo, cloth limp, **2s. 6d.**

Advertising, A History of, from the Earliest Times. Illustrated by Anecdotes, Curious Specimens, and Notices of Successful Advertisers. By HENRY SAMPSON. Crown 8vo, with Coloured Frontispiece and Illustrations, cloth gilt, **7s. 6d.**

Agony Column (The) of "The Times," from 1800 to 1870. Edited, with an Introduction, by ALICE CLAY. Post 8vo, cloth limp, **2s. 6d.**

Aide (Hamilton), Works by:

Carr of Carrlyon. Post 8vo, illustrated boards, **2s.**

Confidences. Post 8vo, illustrated boards, **2s.**

Alexander (Mrs.).—Maid, Wife, or Widow? A Romance. By Mrs. ALEXANDER. Post 8vo, illustrated boards, **2s.**; cr. 8vo, cloth extra, **3s. 6d.**

Allen (Grant), Works by:

Colin Clout's Calendar. Crown 8vo, cloth extra, **6s.**

The Evolutionist at Large. Crown 8vo, cloth extra, **6s.**

Vignettes from Nature. Crown 8vo, cloth extra, **6s.**

Architectural Styles, A Handbook of. Translated from the German of A. ROSENGARTEN, by W. COLLETT-SANDARS. Crown 8vo, cloth extra, with 639 Illustrations, **7s. 6d.**

Art (The) of Amusing: A Collection of Graceful Arts, Games, Tricks, Puzzles, and Charades. By FRANK BELLEW. With 300 Illustrations. Cr. 8vo, cloth extra, **4s. 6d.**

Artemus Ward:

Artemus Ward's Works: The Works of CHARLES FARRER BROWNE, better known as ARTEMUS WARD. With Portrait and Facsimile. Crown 8vo, cloth extra, **7s. 6d.**

Artemus Ward's Lecture on the Mormons. With 32 Illustrations. Edited, with Preface, by EDWARD P. HINGSTON. Crown 8vo, **6d.**

The Genial Showman: Life and Adventures of Artemus Ward. By EDWARD P. HINGSTON. With a Frontispiece. Crown 8vo, cloth extra, **3s. 6d.**

Ashton (John), Works by :

A History of the Chap-Books of the Eighteenth Century. With nearly 400 Illustrations, engraved in facsimile of the originals. Crown 8vo, cloth extra, 7s. 6d.

Social Life in the Reign of Queen Anne. Taken from Original Sources. With nearly 100 Illusts. New and cheaper Ed., cr. 8vo, cl. extra, 7s. 6d.

Humour, Wit, and Satire of the Seventeenth Century. With nearly 100 Illustrations. Crown 8vo, cloth extra, 7s. 6d.

English Caricature and Satire on Napoleon the First. With 120 Illustrations from the Originals. Two Vols., demy 8vo, 28s. [*In preparation.*

Bacteria: A Synopsis of the Bacteria and Yeast Fungi and Allied Species. By W. B. Grove, B.A. With numerous Illustrations. Cr. 8vo, cloth extra, 3s. 6d.   [*In preparation.*

Balzac's "Comedie Humaine" and its Author. With Translations by H. H. Walker. Post 8vo, cl.limp, 2s. 6d.

Bankers, A Handbook of London; together with Lists of Bankers from 1677. By F. G. Hilton Price. Crown 8vo, cloth extra, 7s. 6d.

Bardsley (Rev. C.W.),Works by:

English Surnames: Their Sources and Significations. Cr.8vo, cl. extra, 7s.6d.

Curiosities of Puritan Nomenclature. Crown 8vo, cloth extra, 7s. 6d.

Bartholomew Fair, Memoirs of. By Henry Morley. A New Edition, with One Hundred Illustrations. Crown 8vo, cloth extra, 7s. 6d.

Beauchamp. — Grantley Grange: A Novel. By Shelsley Beauchamp. Post 8vo, illust. bds., 2s.

Beautiful Pictures by British Artists: A Gathering of Favourites from our Picture Galleries. In Two Series. All engraved on Steel in the highest style of Art. Edited, with Notices of the Artists, by Sydney Armytage, M.A. Imperial 4to, cloth extra, gilt and gilt edges, 21s. per Vol.

Bechstein. — As Pretty as Seven, and other German Stories. Collected by Ludwig Bechstein. With Additional Tales by the Brothers Grimm, and 100 Illusts. by Richter. Small 4to, green and gold, 6s. 6d.; gilt edges, 7s. 6d.

Beerbohm. — Wanderings in Patagonia ; or, Life among the Ostrich Hunters. By Julius Beerbohm. With Illusts. Crown 8vo, cloth extra, 3s. 6d.

Belgravia for 1884. One Shilling Monthly. Illustrated. — Two New Serial Stories will begin in the January Number: "The Lover's Creed," by Mrs. Cashel Hoey, Illustrated by P. Macnab ; and "The Wearing of the Green," by the Author of " Love the Debt." In addition to other short stories, the Number will include a complete Story by Wilkie Collins, entitled "She Loves and Lies."

*** *Now ready, the Volume for* July *to* October, 1883, *cloth extra, gilt edges,* 7s. 6d.; *Cases for binding Vols.,* 2s. *each.*

Belgravia Annual : Christmas, 1883. With Stories by James Payn, F. W. Robinson, Dutton Cook, J. Arbuthnot Wilson, and others. Demy 8vo, with Illustrations, 1s.

Bennett (W.C.,LL.D.),Works by:

A Ballad History of England. Post 8vo, cloth limp, 2s.

Songs for Sailors. Post 8vo, cloth limp, 2s.

Besant (Walter) and James Rice, Novels by. Each in post 8vo, illust. boards, 2s. ; cloth limp, 2s. 6d.; or crown 8vo, cloth extra, 3s. 6d.

Ready-Money Mortiboy.

With Harp and Crown.

This Son of Vulcan.

My Little Girl.

The Case of Mr. Lucraft.

The Golden Butterfly.

By Celia's Arbour.

The Monks of Thelema.

'Twas in Trafalgar's Bay.

The Seamy Side.

The Ten Years' Tenant.

The Chaplain of the Fleet.

Besant (Walter), Novels by:

All Sorts and Conditions of Men: An Impossible Story. With Illustrations by Fred. Barnard. Crown 8vo, cloth extra, 3s. 6d.

The Captains' Room, &c. With Frontispiece by E. J. Wheeler. Crown 8vo, cloth extra, 3s. 6d.

All in a Garden Fair. Three Vols., crown 8vo, 31s. 6d.

Birthday Books:—

The Starry Heavens: A Poetical Birthday Book. Square 8vo, handsomely bound in cloth, **2s. 6d.**

Birthday Flowers: Their Language and Legends. By W. J. Gordon. Beautifully Illustrated in Colours by Viola Boughton. In illuminated cover, crown 4to, **6s.**

The Lowell Birthday Book. With Illusts., small 8vo, cloth extra, **4s. 6d.**

Bishop.—Old Mexico, and her Lost Provinces. A Journey in Mexico, Southern California, and Arizona, by way of Cuba. By William Henry Bishop. With nearly 120 fine Woodcut Illustrations. Demy 8vo, cloth extra, **10s. 6d.**

Blackburn's (Henry) Art Handbooks. Demy 8vo, Illustrated, uniform in size for binding.

Academy Notes, separate years, from 1875 to 1882, each **1s.**

Academy Notes, 1883. With Illustrations. **1s.**

Academy Notes, 1875-79. Complete in One Volume, with nearly 600 Illustrations in Facsimile. Demy 8vo, cloth limp, **6s.**

Grosvenor Notes, 1877. **6d.**

Grosvenor Notes, separate years, from 1878 to 1882, each **1s.**

Grosvenor Notes, 1883. With Illustrations. **1s.**

Grosvenor Notes, 1877-82. With upwards of 300 Illustrations. Demy 8vo, cloth limp, **6s.**

Pictures at South Kensington. With 70 Illustrations. **1s.**

The English Pictures at the National Gallery. 114 Illustrations. **1s.**

The Old Masters at the National Gallery. 128 Illustrations. **1s. 6d.**

A Complete Illustrated Catalogue to the National Gallery. With Notes by H. Blackburn, and 242 Illusts. Demy 8vo, cloth limp, **3s.**

The Paris Salon, 1883. With over 300 Illusts. Edited by F. G. Dumas. (English Edition.) Demy 8vo, **3s.**

At the Paris Salon. Sixteen large Plates, printed in facsimile of the Artists' Drawings, in two tints. Edited by F. G. Dumas. Large folio, **1s.**

The Art Annual, 1882-3. Edited by F. G. Dumas. Demy 8vo, **3s. 6d.**

The Art Annual, 1883-4. Edited by F. G. Dumas. With 300 full-page Illustrations. Demy 8vo, **5s.**

Blake (William): Etchings from his Works. By W. B. Scott. With descriptive Text. Folio, half-bound boards, India Proofs, **21s.**

Boccaccio's Decameron; or, Ten Days' Entertainment. Translated into English, with an Introduction by Thomas Wright, F.S.A. With Portrait, and Stothard's beautiful Copperplates. Cr. 8vo, cloth extra, gilt, **7s. 6d.**

Bowers'(G.) Hunting Sketches:

Canters in Crampshire. Oblong 4to, half-bound boards, **21s.**

Leaves from a Hunting Journal. Coloured in facsimile of the originals. Oblong 4to, half-bound, **21s.**

Boyle (Frederick), Works by:

Camp Notes: Stories of Sport and Adventure in Asia, Africa, and America. Crown 8vo, cloth extra, **3s. 6d.**; post 8vo, illustrated bds., **2s.**

Savage Life. Crown 8vo, cloth extra, **3s. 6d.**; post 8vo, illustrated bds., **2s.**

Brand's Observations on Popular Antiquities, chiefly Illustrating the Origin of our Vulgar Customs, Ceremonies, and Superstitions. With the Additions of Sir Henry Ellis. Crown 8vo, cloth extra, gilt, with numerous Illustrations, **7s. 6d.**

Bret Harte, Works by:

Bret Harte's Collected Works. Arranged and Revised by the Author. Complete in Five Vols., crown 8vo, cloth extra, **6s.** each.

Vol. I. Complete Poetical and Dramatic Works. With Steel Plate Portrait, and an Introduction by the Author.

Vol. II. Earlier Papers—Luck of Roaring Camp, and other Sketches —Bohemian Papers — Spanish and American Legends.

Vol. III. Tales of the Argonauts —Eastern Sketches.

Vol. IV. Gabriel Conroy.

Vol. V. Stories — Condensed Novels, &c.

The Select Works of Bret Harte, in Prose and Poetry. With Introductory Essay by J. M. Bellew, Portrait of the Author, and 50 Illustrations. Crown 8vo, cloth extra, **7s. 6d.**

Gabriel Conroy: A Novel. Post 8vo, illustrated boards, **2s.**

An Heiress of Red Dog, and other Stories. Post 8vo, illustrated boards, **2s.**; cloth limp, **2s. 6d.**

The Twins of Table Mountain. Fcap. 8vo, picture cover, **1s.**; crown 8vo, cloth extra, **3s. 6d.**

Luck of Roaring Camp, and other Sketches. Post 8vo, illust. bds., **2s.**

Jeff Briggs's Love Story. Fcap 8vo, picture cover, **1s.**; cloth extra, **2s. 6d.**

Flip. Post 8vo, illustrated boards, **2s.**; cloth limp, **2s. 6d.**

Brewer (Rev. Dr.), Works by:

The Reader's Handbook of Allusions, References, Plots, and Stories. Third Edition, revised throughout, with a New Appendix, containing a COMPLETE ENGLISH BIBLIOGRAPHY. Crown 8vo, 1,400 pages, cloth extra, 7s. 6d.

A Dictionary of Miracles: Imitative, Realistic, and Dogmatic. Crown 8vo, cloth extra, 7s. 6d. [In preparation.

Buchanan's (Robert) Works:

Ballads of Life, Love, and Humour. With a Frontispiece by ARTHUR HUGHES. Crown 8vo, cloth extra, 6s.

Selected Poems of Robert Buchanan. With Frontispiece by T. DALZIEL. Crown 8vo, cloth extra, 6s.

Undertones. Crown 8vo, cloth extra, 6s.

London Poems. Crown 8vo, cloth extra, 6s.

The Book of Orm. Crown 8vo, cloth extra, 6s.

White Rose and Red: A Love Story. Crown 8vo, cloth extra, 6s.

Idylls and Legends of Inverburn. Crown 8vo, cloth extra, 6s.

St. Abe and his Seven Wives: A Tale of Salt Lake City. With a Frontispiece by A. B. HOUGHTON. Crown 8vo, cloth extra, 5s.

The Hebrid Isles: Wanderings in the Land of Lorne and the Outer Hebrides. With Frontispiece by W. SMALL. Crown 8vo, cloth extra, 6s.

A Poet's Sketch-Book: Selections from the Prose Writings of ROBERT BUCHANAN. Crown 8vo, cl. extra, 6s.

Robert Buchanan's Complete Poetical Works. Crown 8vo, cloth extra, 7s. 6d. [In preparation.

The Shadow of the Sword: A Romance. Crown 8vo, cloth extra, 3s. 6d.; post 8vo, illust. boards, 2s.

A Child of Nature: A Romance. With a Frontispiece. Crown 8vo, cloth extra, 3s. 6d.; post 8vo, illust. bds., 2s.

God and the Man: A Romance. With Illustrations by FRED. BARNARD. Crown 8vo, cloth extra, 3s. 6d.

The Martyrdom of Madeline: A Romance. With Frontispiece by A.W. COOPER. Cr. 8vo, cloth extra, 3s. 6d.

Love Me for Ever. With a Frontispiece by P. MACNAB. Crown 8vo, cloth extra, 3s. 6d.

Annan Water: A Romance. Three Vols., crown 8vo.

The New Abelard: A Romance. Three Vols., crown 8vo. [Shortly.

Brewster (Sir David), Works by:

More Worlds than One: The Creed of the Philosopher and the Hope of the Christian. With Plates. Post 8vo, cloth extra, 4s. 6d.

The Martyrs of Science: Lives of GALILEO, TYCHO BRAHE, and KEPLER. With Portraits. Post 8vo, cloth extra, 4s. 6d.

Letters on Natural Magic. A New Edition, with numerous Illustrations, and Chapters on the Being and Faculties of Man, and Additional Phenomena of Natural Magic, by J.A. SMITH. Post 8vo, cloth extra, 4s. 6d.

Brillat-Savarin.—Gastronomy

as a Fine Art. By BRILLAT-SAVARIN. Translated by R. E. ANDERSON, M.A. Post 8vo, cloth limp, 2s. 6d.

Browning.—The Pied Piper of

Hamelin. By ROBERT BROWNING. Illust. by GEORGE CARLINE. Large 4to, illum. cover, 1s. [In preparation.

Burnett (Mrs.), Novels by:

Surly Tim, and other Stories. Post 8vo, illustrated boards, 2s.

Kathleen Mavourneen. Fcap. 8vo, picture cover, 1s.

Lindsay's Luck. Fcap. 8vo, picture cover, 1s.

Pretty Polly Pemberton. Fcap. 8vo, picture cover, 1s.

Burton (Robert):

The Anatomy of Melancholy. A New Edition, complete, corrected and enriched by Translations of the Classical Extracts. Demy 8vo, cloth extra, 7s. 6d.

Melancholy Anatomised: Being an Abridgment, for popular use, of BURTON's ANATOMY OF MELANCHOLY. Post 8vo, cloth limp, 2s. 6d.

Burton (Captain), Works by:

To the Gold Coast for Gold: A Personal Narrative. By RICHARD F. BURTON and VERNEY LOVETT CAMERON. With Maps and Frontispiece. Two Vols., crown 8vo, cloth extra, 21s.

The Book of the Sword: Being a History of the Sword and its Use in all Countries, from the Earliest Times. By RICHARD F. BURTON. With over 400 Illustrations. Square 8vo, cloth extra, 32s. [In preparation.

Bunyan's Pilgrim's Progress.

Edited by Rev. T. SCOTT. With 17 Steel Plates by STOTHARD, engraved by GOODALL, and numerous Woodcuts. Crown 8vo, cloth extra, gilt, 7s. 6d.

Byron (Lord):
Byron's Letters and Journals. With Notices of his Life. By THOMAS MOORE. A Reprint of the Original Edition, newly revised, with Twelve full-page Plates. Crown 8vo, cloth extra, gilt, 7s. 6d.

Byron's Don Juan. Complete in One Vol., post 8vo, cloth limp, 2s.

Cameron (Commander) and Captain Burton.—To the Gold Coast for Gold: A Personal Narrative. By RICHARD F. BURTON and VERNEY LOVETT CAMERON. With Frontispiece and Maps. Two Vols., crown 8vo, cloth extra, 21s.

Cameron (Mrs. H. Lovett), Novels by:
Juliet's Guardian. Post 8vo, illustrated boards, 2s.; crown 8vo, cloth extra, 3s. 6d.

Deceivers Ever. Post 8vo, illustrated boards, 2s.; crown 8vo, cloth extra, 3s. 6d.

Campbell.—White and Black: Travels in the United States. By Sir GEORGE CAMPBELL, M.P. Demy 8vo, cloth extra, 14s.

Carlyle (Thomas):
Thomas Carlyle: Letters and Recollections. By MONCURE D. CONWAY, M.A. Crown 8vo, cloth extra, with Illustrations, 6s.

On the Choice of Books. By THOMAS CARLYLE. With a Life of the Author by R. H. SHEPHERD. New and Revised Edition, post 8vo, cloth extra, Illustrated, 1s. 6d.

The Correspondence of Thomas Carlyle and Ralph Waldo Emerson, 1834 to 1872. Edited by CHARLES ELIOT NORTON. With Portraits. Two Vols., crown 8vo, cloth extra, 24s.

Century (A) of Dishonour: A Sketch of the United States Government's Dealings with some of the Indian Tribes. Crown 8vo, cloth extra, 7s. 6d.

Chapman's (George) Works:
Vol. I. contains the Plays complete, including the doubtful ones. Vol. II., the Poems and Minor Translations, with an Introductory Essay by ALGERNON CHARLES SWINBURNE. Vol. III., the Translations of the Iliad and Odyssey. Three Vols., crown 8vo, cloth extra, 18s.; or separately, 6s. each.

Chatto & Jackson.—A Treatise on Wood Engraving, Historical and Practical. By WM. ANDREW CHATTO and JOHN JACKSON. With an Additional Chapter by HENRY G. BOHN; and 450 fine Illustrations. A Reprint of the last Revised Edition. Large 4to, half-bound, 28s.

Chaucer:
Chaucer for Children: A Golden Key. By Mrs. H. R. HAWEIS. With Eight Coloured Pictures and numerous Woodcuts by the Author. New Ed., small 4to, cloth extra, 6s.

Chaucer for Schools. By Mrs. H. R. HAWEIS. Demy 8vo, cloth limp, 2s. 6d.

Cobban.—The Cure of Souls: A Story. By J. MACLAREN COBBAN. Post 8vo, illustrated boards, 2s.

Collins (C. Allston).—The Bar Sinister: A Story. By C. ALLSTON COLLINS. Post 8vo, illustrated boards, 2s.

Collins (Mortimer & Frances), Novels by:
Sweet and Twenty. Post 8vo, illustrated boards, 2s.

Frances. Post 8vo, illust. bds., 2s.

Blacksmith and Scholar. Post 8vo, illustrated boards, 2s.; crown 8vo, cloth extra, 3s. 6d.

The Village Comedy. Post 8vo, illust. boards, 2s.; cr. 8vo, cloth extra, 3s. 6d.

You Play Me False. Post 8vo, illust. boards, 2s.; cr. 8vo, cloth extra, 3s. 6d.

Collins (Mortimer), Novels by:
Sweet Anne Page. Post 8vo, illustrated boards, 2s.; crown 8vo, cloth extra, 3s. 6d.

Transmigration. Post 8vo, illustrated boards, 2s.; crown 8vo, cloth extra, 3s. 6d.

From Midnight to Midnight. Post 8vo, illustrated boards, 2s.; crown 8vo, cloth extra, 3s. 6d.

A Fight with Fortune. Post 8vo, illustrated boards, 2s.

Colman's Humorous Works: "Broad Grins," "My Nightgown and Slippers," and other Humorous Works, Prose and Poetical, of GEORGE COLMAN. With Life by G. B. BUCKSTONE, and Frontispiece by HOGARTH. Crown 8vo, cloth extra, gilt, 7s. 6d.

Collins (Wilkie), Novels by.
Each post 8vo, illustrated boards, 2s;
cloth limp, 2s. 6d.; or crown 8vo,
cloth extra, Illustrated, 3s. 6d.

Antonina. Illust. by A. CONCANEN.

Basil. Illustrated by Sir JOHN GIL-
BERT and J. MAHONEY.

Hide and Seek. Illustrated by Sir
JOHN GILBERT and J. MAHONEY.

The Dead Secret. Illustrated by Sir
JOHN GILBERT and A. CONCANEN.

Queen of Hearts Illustrated by Sir
JOHN GILBERT and A. CONCANEN.

My Miscellanies. With Illustrations
by A. CONCANEN, and a Steel-plate
Portrait of WILKIE COLLINS.

The Woman In White. With Illustrations by Sir JOHN GILBERT and
F. A. FRASER.

The Moonstone. With Illustrations
by G. DU MAURIER and F. A. FRASER.

Man and Wife. Illust. by W. SMALL.

Poor Miss Finch. Illustrated by
G. DU MAURIER and EDWARD
HUGHES.

Miss or Mrs.? With Illustrations by
S. L. FILDES and HENRY WOODS.

The New Magdalen. Illustrated by
G. DU MAURIER and C. S. RANDS.

The Frozen Deep. Illustrated by
G. DU MAURIER and J. MAHONEY.

The Law and the Lady. Illustrated
by S. L. FILDES and SYDNEY HALL.

The Two Destinies.

The Haunted Hotel. Illustrated by
ARTHUR HOPKINS.

The Fallen Leaves.

Jezebel's Daughter.

The Black Robe.

**Heart and Science: A Story of the
Present Time.** New and Cheaper
Edition. Crown 8vo, cloth extra,
3s. 6d.

Convalescent Cookery: A
Family Handbook. By CATHERINE
RYAN. Post 8vo, cloth limp, 2s. 6d.

Conway (Moncure D.), Works
by:
Demonology and Devil-Lore. Two
Vols., royal 8vo, with 65 Illusts., 28s.

A Necklace of Stories. Illustrated
by W. J. HENNESSY. Square 8vo,
cloth extra, 6s.

The Wandering Jew. Crown 8vo,
cloth extra, 6s.

**Thomas Carlyle: Letters and Re-
collections.** With Illustrations,
Crown 8vo, cloth extra, 6s.

Cook (Dutton), Works by:
Hours with the Players. With a
Steel Plate Frontispiece. New and
Cheaper Edit., cr. 8vo, cloth extra, 6s.

**Nights at the Play: A View of the
English Stage.** New and Cheaper
Edition. Crown 8vo, cloth extra, 6s.

Leo: A Novel. Post 8vo, illustrated
boards, 2s.

Paul Foster's Daughter. Post 8vo,
illustrated boards, 2s.; crown 8vo,
cloth extra, 3s. 6d.

Copyright. — A Handbook of
English and Foreign Copyright in
Literary and Dramatic Works. By
SIDNEY JERROLD, of the Middle
Temple, Esq., Barrister-at-Law. Post
8vo, cloth limp, 2s. 6d.

Cornwall.—Popular Romances
of the West of England; or, The
Drolls, Traditions, and Superstitions
of Old Cornwall. Collected and Edited
by ROBERT HUNT, F.R.S. New and
Revised Edition, with Additions, and
Two Steel-plate Illustrations by
GEORGE CRUIKSHANK. Crown 8vo,
cloth extra, 7s. 6d.

Creasy.—Memoirs of Eminent
Etonians: with Notices of the Early
History of Eton College. By Sir
EDWARD CREASY, Author of "The
Fifteen Decisive Battles of the World."
Crown 8vo, cloth extra, gilt, with 13
Portraits, 7s. 6d.

Cruikshank (George):
The Comic Almanack. Complete in
Two SERIES: The FIRST from 1835
to 1843; the SECOND from 1844 to
1853. A Gathering of the BEST
HUMOUR of THACKERAY, HOOD, MAY-
HEW, ALBERT SMITH, A'BECKETT,
ROBERT BROUGH, &c. With 2,000
Woodcuts and Steel Engravings by
CRUIKSHANK, HINE, LANDELLS, &c.
Crown 8vo, cloth gilt, two very thick
volumes, 7s. 6d. each.

The Life of George Cruikshank. By
BLANCHARD JERROLD, Author of
"The Life of Napoleon III.," &c.
With 84 Illustrations. New and
Cheaper Edition, enlarged, with Ad-
ditional Plates, and a very carefully
compiled Bibliography. Crown 8vo,
cloth extra, 7s. 6d.

Robinson Crusoe. A choicely-printed
Edition, with 37 Woodcuts and Two
Steel Plates, by GEORGE CRUIK-
SHANK. Crown 8vo, cloth extra, 7s. 6d.
100 Large Paper copies, carefully
printed on hand-made paper, with
India proofs of the Illustrations,
price 36s.

Cumming.—In the Hebrides.
By C. F. GORDON CUMMING, Author
of "At Home in Fiji." With Autotype Facsimile and Illustrations. Demy
8vo, cloth extra, 8s. 6d.

Cussans.—Handbook of Her-
aldry; with Instructions for Tracing
Pedigrees and Deciphering Ancient
MSS., &c. By JOHN E. CUSSANS.
Entirely New and Revised Edition,
illustrated with over 400 Woodcuts
and Coloured Plates. Crown 8vo,
cloth extra, 7s. 6d.

Cyples.—Hearts of Gold: A
Novel. By WILLIAM CYPLES. Crown
8vo, cloth extra, 3s. 6d.

Daniel. — Merrie England in
the Olden Time. By GEORGE DANIEL.
With Illustrations by ROBT. CRUIK-
SHANK. Crown 8vo, cloth extra, 3s. 6d.

Daudet.—Port Salvation; or,
The Evangelist. By ALPHONSE
DAUDET. Translated by C. HARRY
MELTZER. With Portrait of the
Author. Crown 8vo, cloth extra,
3s. 6d.

Davenant. — What shall my
Son be? Hints for Parents on the
Choice of a Profession or Trade for
their Sons. By FRANCIS DAVENANT,
M.A. Post 8vo, cloth limp, 2s. 6d.

Davies' (Sir John) Complete
Poetical Works, including Psalms I.
to L. in Verse, and other hitherto Un-
published MSS., for the first time
Collected and Edited, with Memorial-
Introduction and Notes, by the Rev.
A. B. GROSART, D.D. Two Vols.,
crown 8vo, cloth boards, 12s.

De Maistre.—A Journey Round
My Room. By XAVIER DE MAISTRE.
Translated by HENRY ATTWELL. Post
8vo, cloth limp, 2s. 6d.

De Mille.—A Castle in Spain.
A Novel. By JAMES DE MILLE. With
a Frontispiece. Crown 8vo, cloth
extra, 3s. 6d.

Derwent (Leith), Novels by:
Our Lady of Tears. Cr. 8vo, cloth
extra, 3s. 6d.; post 8vo, illust. bds., 2s.
Circe's Lovers. Crown 8vo, cloth
extra, 3s. 6d. [In preparation.

Dickens (Charles), Novels by:
Post 8vo, illustrated boards, 2s. each.
Sketches by Boz. | Nicholas Nickleby.
Pickwick Papers. | Oliver Twist.

The Speeches of Charles Dickens.
(Mayfair Library.) Post 8vo, cloth
limp, 2s. 6d.

The Speeches of Charles Dickens,
1841-1870. With a New Bibliography,
revised and enlarged. Edited and
Prefaced by RICHARD HERNE SHEP-
HERD. Crown 8vo, cloth extra, 6s.

About England with Dickens. By
ALFRED RIMMER. With 57 Illustrations by C. A. VANDERHOOF, ALFRED
RIMMER, and others. Sq. 8vo, cloth
extra, 10s. 6d.

Dictionaries:

A Dictionary of Miracles: Imitative,
Realistic, and Dogmatic. By the
Rev. E. C. BREWER, LL.D. Crown
8vo, cloth extra, 7s. 6d. [Preparing.

A Dictionary of the Drama: Being
a comprehensive Guide to the Plays,
Playwrights, Players, and Playhouses
of the United Kingdom and America,
from the Earliest to the Present
Times. By W. DAVENPORT ADAMS.
A thick volume, crown 8vo, half-
bound, 12s. 6d. [In preparation.

Familiar Allusions: A Handbook
of Miscellaneous Information; including the Names of Celebrated
Statues, Paintings, Palaces, Country
Seats, Ruins, Churches, Ships,
Streets, Clubs, Natural Curiosities,
and the like. By WM. A. WHEELER
and CHARLES G. WHEELER. Demy
8vo, cloth extra, 7s. 6d.

The Reader's Handbook of Allu-
sions, References, Plots, and
Stories. By the Rev. E. C. BREWER,
LL.D. Third Edition, revised
throughout, with a New Appendix,
containing a Complete English Bibliography. Crown 8vo, 1,400 pages,
cloth extra, 7s. 6d.

Short Sayings of Great Men. With
Historical and Explanatory Notes.
By SAMUEL A. BENT, M.A. Demy
8vo, cloth extra, 7s. 6d.

The Slang Dictionary: Etymological,
Historical, and Anecdotal. Crown
8vo, cloth extra, 6s. 6d.

Words, Facts, and Phrases: A Dictionary of Curious, Quaint, and Out-
of-the-Way Matters. By ELIEZER
EDWARDS. Crown 8vo, half-bound,
12s. 6d.

Dobson (W. T.), Works by :
Literary Frivolities, Fancies, Follies, and Frolics. Post 8vo, cloth limp, 2s. 6d.
Poetical Ingenuities and Eccentricities. Post 8vo, cloth limp, 2s. 6d.

Doran. — Memories of our Great Towns ; with Anecdotic Gleanings concerning their Worthies and their Oddities. By Dr. JOHN DORAN, F.S.A. With 38 Illustrations. New and Cheaper Edition, crown 8vo, cloth extra, 7s. 6d.

Drama, A Dictionary of the. Being a comprehensive Guide to the Plays, Playwrights, Players, and Playhouses of the United Kingdom and America, from the Earliest to the Present Times. By W. DAVENPORT ADAMS. (Uniform with BREWER'S "Reader's Handbook.") Crown 8vo, half-bound, 12s. 6d. [*In preparation.*

Dramatists, The Old. Crown 8vo, cloth extra, with Vignette Portraits, 6s. per Vol.
Ben Jonson's Works. With Notes Critical and Explanatory, and a Biographical Memoir by WM. GIFFORD. Edited by Colonel CUNNINGHAM. Three Vols.
Chapman's Works. Complete in Three Vols. Vol. I. contains the Plays complete, including the doubtful ones ; Vol. II., the Poems and Minor Translations, with an Introductory Essay by ALGERNON CHAS. SWINBURNE ; Vol. III., the Translations of the Iliad and Odyssey.
Marlowe's Works. Including his Translations. Edited, with Notes and Introduction, by Col. CUNNINGHAM. One Vol.
Massinger's Plays. From the Text of WILLIAM GIFFORD. Edited by Col. CUNNINGHAM. One Vol.

Dyer. — The Folk - Lore of Plants. By T. F. THISELTON DYER, M.A. Crown 8vo, cloth extra, 6s. [*In preparation.*

Edwards, Betham-. — Felicia : A Novel. By M. BETHAM-EDWARDS. Post 8vo, illustrated boards, 2s. ; crown 8vo, cloth extra, 3s. 6d.

Edwardes (Mrs. A.), Novels by :
A Point of Honour. Post 8vo, illustrated boards, 2s.
Archie Lovell. Post 8vo, illust. bds., 2s. ; crown 8vo, cloth extra, 3s. 6d.

Early English Poets. Edited, with Introductions and Annotations, by Rev. A. B. GROSART, D.D. Crown 8vo, cloth boards, 6s. per Volume.
Fletcher's (Giles, B.D.) Complete Poems. One Vol.
Davies' (Sir John) Complete Poetical Works. Two Vols.
Herrick's (Robert) Complete Collected Poems. Three Vols.
Sidney's (Sir Philip) Complete Poetical Works. Three Vols.

Herbert (Lord) of Cherbury's Poems. Edited, with Introduction, by J. CHURTON COLLINS. Crown 8vo, parchment, 8s.

Eggleston. — Roxy : A Novel. By EDWARD EGGLESTON. Post 8vo, illust. boards, 2s. ; cr. 8vo, cloth extra, 3s. 6d.

Emanuel. — On Diamonds and Precious Stones : their History, Value, and Properties ; with Simple Tests for ascertaining their Reality. By HARRY EMANUEL, F.R.G.S. With numerous Illustrations, tinted and plain. Crown 8vo, cloth extra, gilt, 6s.

Englishman's House, The : A Practical Guide to all interested in Selecting or Building a House, with full Estimates of Cost, Quantities, &c. By C. J. RICHARDSON. Third Edition. With nearly 600 Illustrations. Crown 8vo, cloth extra, 7s. 6d.

Ewald (Alex. Charles, F.S.A.), Works by :
Stories from the State Papers. With an Autotype Facsimile. Crown 8vo, cloth extra, 6s.
The Life and Times of Prince Charles Stuart, Count of Albany, commonly called the Young Pretender. From the State Papers and other Sources. New and Cheaper Edition, with a Portrait, crown 8vo, cloth extra, 7s. 6d.

Eyes, The. — How to Use our Eyes, and How to Preserve Them. By JOHN BROWNING, F.R.A.S., &c. With 37 Illustrations. Crown 8vo, 1s.; cloth, 1s. 6d.

Fairholt. — Tobacco : Its History and Associations ; with an Account of the Plant and its Manufacture, and its Modes of Use in all Ages and Countries. By F. W. FAIRHOLT, F.S.A. With Coloured Frontispiece and upwards of 100 Illustrations by the Author. Crown 8vo, cloth extra, 6s.

Familiar Allusions: A Handbook of Miscellaneous Information; including the Names of Celebrated Statues, Paintings, Palaces, Country Seats, Ruins, Churches, Ships, Streets, Clubs, Natural Curiosities, and the like. By WILLIAM A. WHEELER, Author of " Noted Names of Fiction ; " and CHARLES G. WHEELER. Demy 8vo, cloth extra, 7s. 6d.

Faraday (Michael), Works by:

The Chemical History of a Candle: Lectures delivered before a Juvenile Audience at the Royal Institution. Edited by WILLIAM CROOKES, F.C.S. Post 8vo, cloth extra, with numerous Illustrations, 4s. 6d.

On the Various Forces of Nature, and their Relations to each other: Lectures delivered before a Juvenile Audience at the Royal Institution. Edited by WILLIAM CROOKES, F.C.S. Post 8vo, cloth extra, with numerous Illustrations, 4s. 6d.

Fin-Bec. — The Cupboard Papers: Observations on the Art of Living and Dining. By FIN-BEC. Post 8vo, cloth limp, 2s. 6d.

Fitzgerald (Percy), Works by:

The Recreations of a Literary Man ; or, Does Writing Pay? With Recollections of some Literary Men, and a View of a Literary Man's Working Life. Cr.8vo, cloth extra, 6s.

The World Behind the Scenes. Crown 8vo, cloth extra, 3s. 6d.

Little Essays: Passages from the Letters of CHARLES LAMB. Post 8vo, cloth limp, 2s. 6d.

Post 8vo, illustrated boards, 2s. each.

Bella Donna.
Never Forgotten.
The Second Mrs. Tillotson.
Polly.
Seventy-five Brooke Street.

Fletcher's (Giles, B.D.) Complete Poems: Christ's Victorie in Heaven, Christ's Victorie on Earth, Christ's Triumph over Death, and Minor Poems. With Memorial-Introduction and Notes by the Rev. A. B. GROSART, D.D. Cr. 8vo, cloth bds., 6s.

Fonblanque. — Filthy Lucre: A Novel. By ALBANY DE FONBLANQUE. Post 8vo, illustrated boards, 2s.

French Literature, History of. By HENRY VAN LAUN. Complete in 3 Vols., demy 8vo, cl. bds., 7s. 6d. each.

Francillon (R. E.), Novels by:
Crown 8vo, cloth extra, 3s. 6d. each; post 8vo, illust. boards, 2s. each.

Olympia.
Queen Cophetua.
One by One.

Esther's Glove. Fcap. 8vo, picture cover, 1s.

Frere. — Pandurang Hari ; or, Memoirs of a Hindoo. With a Preface by Sir H. BARTLE-FRERE, G.C.S.I., &c. Crown 8vo, cloth extra, 3s. 6d. ; post 8vo, illustrated boards, 2s.

Frost (Thomas), Works by:
Crown 8vo, cloth extra, 3s. 6d. each.

Circus Life and Circus Celebrities.
The Lives of the Conjurers.
The Old Showmen and the Old London Fairs.

Fry. — Royal Guide to the London Charities, 1883-4. By HERBERT FRY. Showing, in alphabetical order, their Name, Date of Foundation, Address, Objects, Annual Income, Chief Officials, &c. Published Annually. Crown 8vo, cloth, 1s. 6d.

Gardening Books:

A Year's Work In Garden and Greenhouse: Practical Advice to Amateur Gardeners as to the Management of the Flower, Fruit, and Frame Garden. By GEORGE GLENNY. Post 8vo, cloth limp, 2s. 6d.

Our Kitchen Garden. The Plants we Grow, and How we Cook Them. By TOM JERROLD, Author of "The Garden that Paid the Rent," &c. Post 8vo, cloth limp, 2s. 6d.

Household Horticulture: A Gossip about Flowers. By TOM and JANE JERROLD. Illustrated. Post 8vo, cloth limp, 2s. 6d.

The Garden that Paid the Rent. By TOM JERROLD. Fcap. 8vo, illustrated cover, 1s. ; cloth limp, 1s. 6d.

Gentleman's Magazine (The) for 1884. One Shilling Monthly. A New Serial Story, entitled "Phillstla," By CECIL POWER, will be begun in the JANUARY Number. "Science Notes," by W. MATTIEU WILLIAMS, F.R.A.S., will also be continued monthly.

₊ *Now ready, the Volume for* JULY *to* DECEMBER, 1883, *cloth extra, price* 8s. 6d. ; *Cases for binding,* 2s. *each.*

Gentleman's Annual (The). Christmas, 1883. Containing Two Complete Novels by PERCY FITZGERALD and Mrs. ALEXANDER. Demy 8vo, illuminated cover, 1s.

Garrett.—The Capel Girls: A Novel. By EDWARD GARRETT. Post 8vo, illustrated boards, 2s.; crown 8vo, cloth extra, 3s. 6d.

German Popular Stories. Collected by the Brothers GRIMM, and Translated by EDGAR TAYLOR. Edited, with an Introduction, by JOHN RUSKIN. With 22 Illustrations on Steel by GEORGE CRUIKSHANK. Square 8vo, cloth extra, 6s. 6d.; gilt edges, 7s. 6d.

Gibbon (Charles), Novels by:

Each in crown 8vo, cloth extra, 3s. 6d.; or post 8vo, illustrated boards, 2s.

Robin Gray.
For Lack of Gold.
What will the World Say?
In Honour Bound.
In Love and War.
For the King.
Queen of the Meadow.
In Pastures Green.

Post 8vo, illustrated boards, 2s.
The Dead Heart.

Crown 8vo, cloth extra, 3s. 6d. each.
The Braes of Yarrow.
The Flower of the Forest.
A Heart's Problem.
The Golden Shaft.
Of High Degree.

Fancy-Free. Three Vols., crown 8vo, 31s. 6d. [*In the press.*

Gilbert (William), Novels by:

Post 8vo, illustrated boards, 2s. each.
Dr. Austin's Guests.
The Wizard of the Mountain.
James Duke, Costermonger.

Gilbert (W. S.), Original Plays by: In Two Series, each complete in itself, price 2s. 6d. each. FIRST SERIES contains The Wicked World—Pygmalion and Galatea — Charity — The Princess—The Palace of Truth—Trial by Jury. The SECOND SERIES contains Broken Hearts — Engaged — Sweethearts—Gretchen—Dan'l Druce —Tom Cobb—H.M.S. Pinafore—The Sorcerer—The Pirates of Penzance.

Glenny.—A Year's Work in Garden and Greenhouse: Practical Advice to Amateur Gardeners as to the Management of the Flower, Fruit, and Frame Garden. By GEORGE GLENNY. Post 8vo, cloth limp, 2s. 6d.

Godwin.—Lives of the Necro. mancers. By WILLIAM GODWIN. Post 8vo, cloth limp, 2s.

Golden Library, The:
Square 16mo (Tauchnitz size), cloth limp, 2s. per volume.

Bayard Taylor's Diversions of the Echo Club.
Bennett's (Dr. W. C.) Ballad History of England.
Bennett's (Dr. W. C.) Songs for Sailors.
Byron's Don Juan.
Godwin's (William) Lives of the Necromancers.
Holmes's Autocrat of the Breakfast Table. With an Introduction by G. A. SALA.
Holmes's Professor at the Breakfast Table.
Hood's Whims and Oddities. Complete. All the original Illustrations.
Irving's (Washington) Tales of a Traveller.
Irving's (Washington) Tales of the Alhambra.
Jesse's (Edward) Scenes and Occupations of a Country Life.
Lamb's Essays of Elia. Both Series Complete in One Vol.
Leigh Hunt's Essays: A Tale for a Chimney Corner, and other Pieces. With Portrait, and Introduction by EDMUND OLLIER.
Mallory's (Sir Thomas) Mort d'Arthur: The Stories of King Arthur and of the Knights of the Round Table. Edited by B. MONTGOMERIE RANKING.
Pascal's Provincial Letters. A New Translation, with Historical Introduction and Notes, by T. M'CRIE, D.D.
Pope's Poetical Works. Complete.
Rochefoucauld's Maxims and Moral Reflections. With Notes, and Introductory Essay by SAINTE-BEUVE.
St. Pierre's Paul and Virginia, and The Indian Cottage. Edited, with Life, by the Rev. E. CLARKE.
Shelley's Early Poems, and Queen Mab. With Essay by LEIGH HUNT.
Shelley's Later Poems: Laon and Cythna, &c.
Shelley's Posthumous Poems, the Shelley Papers, &c.
Shelley's Prose Works, including A Refutation of Deism, Zastrozzi, St. Irvyne, &c.
White's Natural History of Selborne. Edited, with Additions, by THOMAS BROWN, F.L.S.

Golden Treasury of Thought,
The: An ENCYCLOPÆDIA OF QUOTA-
TIONS from Writers of all Times and
Countries. Selected and Edited by
THEODORE TAYLOR. Crown 8vo, cloth
gilt and gilt edges, 7s. 6d.

Gordon Cumming.— In the
Hebrides. By C. F. GORDON CUMMING,
Author of "At Home in Fiji." With
Autotype Facsimile and numerous
full-page Illustrations. Demy 8vo,
cloth extra, 8s. 6d.

Graham. — The Professor's
Wife: A Story. By LEONARD GRAHAM.
Fcap. 8vo, picture cover, 1s.; cloth
extra, 2s. 6d.

Greeks and Romans, The Life
of the, Described from Antique Monu-
ments. By ERNST GUHL and W.
KONER. Translated from the Third
German Edition, and Edited by Dr.
F. HUEFFER. With 545 Illustrations.
New and Cheaper Edition, demy 8vo,
cloth extra, 7s. 6d.

Greenwood (James),Works by :
The Wilds of London. Crown 8vo,
cloth extra, 3s. 6d.
Low-Life Deeps: An Account of the
Strange Fish to be Found There.
Crown 8vo, cloth extra, 3s. 6d.
Dick Temple: A Novel. Post 8vo,
illustrated boards, 2s.

Guyot.—The Earth and Man ;
or, Physical Geography in its relation
to the History of Mankind. By
ARNOLD GUYOT. With Additions by
Professors AGASSIZ, PIERCE, and GRAY;
12 Maps and Engravings on Steel,
some Coloured, and copious Index.
Crown 8vo, cloth extra, gilt, 4s. 6d.

Hair (The): Its Treatment in
Health, Weakness, and Disease.
Translated from the German of Dr. J.
PINCUS. Crown 8vo, 1s.; cloth, 1s. 6d.

Hake (Dr. Thomas Gordon),
Poems by:
Madien Ecstasy. Small 4to, cloth
extra, 8s.
New Symbols. Crown 8vo, cloth
extra, 6s.
Legends of the Morrow. Crown 8vo,
cloth extra, 6s.
The Serpent Play. Crown 8vo, cloth
extra, 6s.

Hall.—Sketches of Irish Cha-
racter. By Mrs. S. C. HALL. With
numerous Illustrations on Steel and
Wood by MACLISE, GILBERT, HARVEY,
and G. CRUIKSHANK. Medium 8vo,
cloth extra, gilt, 7s. 6d.

Halliday.—Every-day Papers.
By ANDREW HALLIDAY. Post 8vo,
illustrated boards, 2s.

Handwriting, The Philosophy
of. With over 100 Facsimiles and Explanatory Text. By DON FELIX DE
SALAMANCA. Post 8vo, cloth limp,
2s. 6d.

Hanky-Panky : A Collection of
Very EasyTricks,Very Difficult Tricks,
White Magic, Sleight of Hand, &c.
Edited by W. H. CREMER. With 200
Illustrations. Crown 8vo, cloth extra,
4s. 6d.

Hardy (Lady Duffus). — Paul
Wynter's Sacrifice: A Story. By
Lady DUFFUS HARDY. Post 8vo, illust.
boards, 2s.

Hardy (Thomas).—Under the
Greenwood Tree. By THOMAS HARDY,
Author of "Far from the Madding
Crowd." Crown 8vo, cloth extra,
3s. 6d.; post 8vo, illustrated boards,
2s.

Haweis (Mrs. H. R.), Works by :
The Art of Dress. With numerous
Illustrations. Small 8vo, illustrated
cover, 1s.; cloth limp, 1s. 6d.
The Art of Beauty. New and Cheaper
Edition. Crown 8vo, cloth extra,
with Coloured Frontispiece and Il-
lustrations, 6s.
The Art of Decoration. Square 8vo,
handsomely bound and profusely
Illustrated, 10s. 6d.
Chaucer for Children: A Golden
Key. With Eight Coloured Pictures
and numerous Woodcuts. New
Edition, small 4to, cloth extra, 6s.
Chaucer for Schools. Demy 8vo,
cloth limp, 2s. 6d.

Haweis (Rev. H. R.).—American
Humorists. Including WASHINGTON
IRVING, OLIVER WENDELL HOLMES,
JAMES RUSSELL LOWELL, ARTEMUS
WARD,MARK TWAIN, and BRET HARTE.
By the Rev. H. R. HAWEIS, M.A.
Crown 8vo, cloth extra, 6s.

Hawthorne (Julian), Novels by.
Crown 8vo, cloth extra, **3s. 6d.** each;
post 8vo, illustrated boards, **2s.** each.

    Garth.

    Ellice Quentin.

    Sebastian Strome.

Mrs. Gainsborough's Diamonds.
Fcap. 8vo, illustrated cover, **1s.**;
cloth extra, **2s. 6d.**

Prince Saroni's Wife. Crown 8vo,
cloth extra, **3s. 6d.**

Dust: A Novel. Crown 8vo, cloth
extra, **3s. 6d.**

Fortune's Fool. Three Vols., crown
8vo, **31s. 6d.**

Beatrix Randolph. Two Vols., crown
8vo.   [*Shortly.*

Heath (F. G.). — My Garden
Wild, and What I Grew There. By
FRANCIS GEORGE HEATH, Author of
"The Fern World," &c. Crown 8vo,
cloth extra, **5s.**; cloth gilt, and gilt
edges, **6s.**

Helps (Sir Arthur), Works by:

Animals and their Masters. Post
8vo, cloth limp, **2s. 6d.**

Social Pressure. Post 8vo, cloth limp,
2s. 6d.

Ivan de Biron: A Novel. Crown 8vo,
cloth extra, **3s. 6d.**; post 8vo, illustrated boards, **2s.**

Heptalogia (Vhe); or, The
Seven against Sense. A Cap with
Seven Bells. Cr. 8vo, cloth extra, **6s.**

Herbert.—The Poems of Lord
Herbert of Cherbury. Edited, with
an Introduction, by J. CHURTON
COLLINS. Crown 8vo, bound in parchment, **8s.**

Herrick's (Robert) Hesperides,
Noble Numbers, and Complete Collected Poems. With Memorial-Introduction and Notes by the Rev. A. B.
GROSART, D.D., Steel Portrait, Index
of First Lines, and Glossarial Index,
&c. Three Vols., crown 8vo, cloth
boards, **18s.**

Hesse - Wartegg (Chevalier
Ernst von), Works by:

Tunis: The Land and the People.
With 22 Illustrations. Crown 8vo,
cloth extra, **3s. 6d.**

The New South-West: Travelling
Sketches from Kansas, New Mexico,
Arizona, and Northern Mexcio.
With 100 fine Illustrations and 3
Maps. Demy 8vo, cloth extra,
14s.   [*In preparation.*

Hindley (Charles), Works by:
Crown 8vo, cloth extra, **3s. 6d.** each.

Tavern Anecdotes and Sayings: In-
cluding the Origin of Signs, and
Reminiscences connected with
Taverns, Coffee Houses, Clubs, &c.
With Illustrations.

**The Life and Adventures of a Cheap
Jack.** By One of the Fraternity.
Edited by CHARLES HINDLEY.

Holmes (Oliver Wendell), Works
by:

**The Autocrat of the Breakfast-
Table.** Illustrated by J. GORDON
THOMSON. Post 8vo, cloth limp,
2s. 6d.; another Edition in smaller
type, with an Introduction by G. A.
SALA. Post 8vo, cloth limp, **2s.**

**The Professor at the Breakfast-
Table;** with the Story of Iris. Post
8vo, cloth limp, **2s.**

Holmes. — The Science of
Voice Production and Voice Preser-
vation: A Popular Manual for the
Use of Speakers and Singers. By
GORDON HOLMES, M.D. Crown 8vo,
cloth limp, with Illustrations, **2s. 6d.**

Hood (Thomas):

**Hood's Choice Works, in Prose and
Verse.** Including the Cream of the
Comic Annuals. With Life of the
Author, Portrait, and 200 Illustra-
tions. Crown 8vo, cloth extra, **7s. 6d.**

Hood's Whims and Oddities. Complete. With all the original Illustrations. Post 8vo, cloth limp, **2s.**

Hood (Tom), Works by:

From Nowhere to the North Pole:
A Noah's Arkæological Narrative.
With 25 Illustrations by W. BRUN-
TON and E. C. BARNES. Square
crown 8vo, cloth extra, gilt edges, **6s.**

A Golden Heart: A Novel. Post 8vo,
illustrated boards, **2s.**

Hook's (Theodore) Choice Hu-
morous Works, including his Ludi-
crous Adventures, Bons Mots, Puns and
Hoaxes. With a New Life of the
Author, Portraits, Facsimiles, and
Illustrations. Crown 8vo, cloth extra,
gilt, **7s. 6d.**

Horne.—Orion : An Epic Poem,
in Three Books. By RICHARD HEN-
GIST HORNE. With Photographic
Portrait from a Medallion by SUM-
MERS. Tenth Edition, crown 8vo,
cloth extra, **7s.**

Howell.—Conflicts of Capital
and Labour, Historically and Eco-
nomically considered: Being a History and Review of the Trade Unions
of Great Britain, showing their Origin,
Progress, Constitution, and Objects, in
their Political, Social, Economical,
and Industrial Aspects. By GEORGE
HOWELL. Cr. 8vo, cloth extra, 7s. 6d.

Hugo. — The Hunchback of
Notre Dame. By VICTOR HUGO.
Post 8vo, illustrated boards, 2s.

Hunt.—Essays by Leigh Hunt.
A Tale for a Chimney Corner, and
other Pieces. With Portrait and Introduction by EDMUND OLLIER. Post
8vo, cloth limp, 2s.

Hunt (Mrs. Alfred), Novels by:
Thornicroft's Model. Crown 8vo,
cloth extra, 3s. 6d.; post 8vo, illustrated boards, 2s.
The Leaden Casket. Crown 8vo,
cloth extra, 3s. 6d.; post 8vo, illustrated boards, 2s.
Self-Condemned. Crown 8vo, cloth
extra, 3s. 6d.

Ingelow.—Fated to be Free: A
Novel. By JEAN INGELOW. Crown
8vo, cloth extra, 3s. 6d.; post 8vo,
illustrated boards, 2s.

Irish Wit and Humour, Songs
of. Collected and Edited by A. PERCE-
VAL GRAVES. Post 8vo, cloth limp,
2s. 6d. [In preparation.

Irving (Henry).—The Paradox
of Acting. Translated, with Annotations, from Diderot's "Le Paradoxe
sur le Comédien," by WALTER HER-
RIES POLLOCK. With a Preface by
HENRY IRVING. Crown 8vo, in parchment, 4s. 6d.

Irving (Washington),Works by:
Post 8vo, cloth limp, 2s. each.
Tales of a Traveller.
Tales of the Alhambra.

James.—Confidence: A Novel.
By HENRY JAMES, Jun. Crown 8vo,
cloth extra, 3s. 6d.; post 8vo, illustrated boards, 2s.

Janvier.—Practical Keramics
for Students. By CATHERINE A.
JANVIER. Crown 8vo, cloth extra, 6s.

Jay (Harriett), Novels by. Each
crown 8vo, cloth extra, 3s. 6d.; or post
8vo, illustrated boards, 2s.
The Dark Colleen.
The Queen of Connaught.

Jefferies.—Nature near London. By RICHARD JEFFERIES, Author
of "The Gamekeeper at Home."
Crown 8vo, cloth extra, 6s.

Jennings (H. J.).—Curiosities
of Criticism. By HENRY J. JENNINGS.
Post 8vo, cloth limp, 2s. 6d.

Jennings (Hargrave). — The
Rosicrucians: Their Rites and Mysteries. With Chapters on the Ancient
Fire and Serpent Worshippers. By
HARGRAVE JENNINGS. With Five full-
page Plates and upwards of 300 Illustrations. A New Edition, crown 8vo,
cloth extra, 7s. 6d.

Jerrold (Tom), Works by:
The Garden that Paid the Rent.
By TOM JERROLD. Fcap. 8vo, illus-
trated cover, 1s.; cloth limp, 1s. 6d.
Household Horticulture: A Gossip
about Flowers. By TOM and JANE
JERROLD. Illustrated. Post 8vo,
cloth limp, 2s. 6d.
Our Kitchen Garden: The Plants
we Grow, and How we Cook Them.
By TOM JERROLD. Post 8vo, cloth
limp, 2s. 6d.

Jesse.—Scenes and Occupa-
tions of a Country Life. By EDWARD
JESSE. Post 8vo, cloth limp, 2s.

Jones (Wm., F.S.A.), Works by:
Finger-Ring Lore: Historical, Le-
gendary, and Anecdotal. With over
200 Illustrations. Crown 8vo, cloth
extra, 7s. 6d.
Credulities, Past and Present; including the Sea and Seamen, Miners,
Talismans,Word and Letter Divina-
tion, Exorcising and Blessing of
Animals, Birds, Eggs, Luck, &c.
With an Etched Frontispiece. Crown
8vo, cloth extra, 7s. 6d.
Crowns and Coronations: A History
of Regalia in all Times and Countries. With One Hundred Illustrations. Cr. 8vo, cloth extra, 7s. 6d.

Jonson's (Ben) Works. With
Notes Critical and Explanatory, and
a Biographical Memoir by WILLIAM
GIFFORD. Edited by Colonel CUN-
NINGHAM. Three Vols., crown 8vo,
cloth extra, 18s.; or separately, 6s. each.

Josephus,TheCompleteWorks
of. Translated by WHISTON. Containing both "The Antiquities of the
Jews" and "The Wars of the Jews."
Two Vols., 8vo, with 52 Illustrations
and Maps, cloth extra, gilt, 14s.

Kavanagh.—The Pearl Fountain, and other Fairy Stories. By BRIDGET and JULIA KAVANAGH. With Thirty Illustrations by J. MOYR SMITH. Small 8vo, cloth gilt, 6s.

Kempt.—Pencil and Palette: Chapters on Art and Artists. By ROBERT KEMPT. Post 8vo, cloth limp, 2s. 6d.

Kingsley (Henry), Novels by: Each crown 8vo, cloth extra, 3s. 6d.; or post 8vo, illustrated boards, 2s.

　Oakshott Castle.
　Number Seventeen.

Lamb (Charles):

Mary and Charles Lamb: Their Poems, Letters, and Remains. With Reminiscences and Notes by W. CAREW HAZLITT. With HANCOCK'S Portrait of the Essayist, Facsimiles of the Title-pages of the rare First Editions of Lamb's and Coleridge's Works, and numerous Illustrations. Crown 8vo, cloth extra, 10s. 6d.

Lamb's Complete Works, in Prose and Verse, reprinted from the Original Editions, with many Pieces hitherto unpublished. Edited, with Notes and Introduction, by R. H. SHEPHERD. With Two Portraits and Facsimile of Page of the "Essay on Roast Pig." Cr. 8vo, cloth extra, 7s. 6d.

The Essays of Elia. Complete Edition. Post 8vo, cloth extra, 2s.

Poetry for Children, and Prince Dorus. By CHARLES LAMB. Carefully Reprinted from unique copies. Small 8vo, cloth extra, 5s.

Little Essays: Passages from the Letters of CHARLES LAMB. Selected and Edited by PERCY FITZGERALD. Post 8vo, cloth limp, 2s. 6d.

Lares and Penates; or, The Background of Life. By FLORENCE CADDY. Crown 8vo, cloth extra, 6s.

Lane's Arabian Nights, &c.:

The Thousand and One Nights: commonly called, in England, "THE ARABIAN NIGHTS' ENTERTAINMENTS." A New Translation from the Arabic, with copious Notes, by EDWARD WILLIAM LANE. Illustrated by many hundred Engravings on Wood, from Original Designs by WM. HARVEY. A New Edition, from a Copy annotated by the Translator, edited by his Nephew, EDWARD STANLEY POOLE. With a Preface by STANLEY LANE-POOLE. Three Vols., demy 8vo, cloth extra, 7s. 6d. each.

Lane's Arabian Nights, &c.

Arabian Society in the Middle Ages: Studies from "The Thousand and One Nights." By EDWARD WILLIAM LANE, Author of "The Modern Egyptians," &c. Edited by STANLEY LANE-POOLE. Crown 8vo, cloth extra, 6s.

Larwood (Jacob), Works by:

The Story of the London Parks. With Illustrations. Crown 8vo, cloth extra, 3s. 6d.

Clerical Anecdotes. Post 8vo, cloth limp, 2s. 6d.

Forensic Anecdotes. Post 8vo, cloth limp, 2s. 6d.

Theatrical Anecdotes. Post 8vo, cloth limp, 2s. 6d.

Leigh (Henry S.), Works by:

Carols of Cockayne. With numerous Illustrations. Post 8vo, cloth limp, 2s. 6d.

Jeux d'Esprit. Collected and Edited by HENRY S. LEIGH. Post 8vo, cloth limp, 2s. 6d.

Life In London; or, The History of Jerry Hawthorn and Corinthian Tom. With the whole of CRUIKSHANK'S Illustrations, in Colours, after the Originals. Crown 8vo, cloth extra, 7s. 6d.

Linton (E. Lynn), Works by:

Witch Stories. Post 8vo, cloth limp, 2s. 6d.

The True Story of Joshua Davidson. Post 8vo, cloth limp, 2s. 6d.

Crown 8vo, cloth extra, 3s. 6d. each; post 8vo, illustrated boards, 2s.

　Patricia Kemball.
　The Atonement of Leam Dundas.
　The World Well Lost.
　Under which Lord?
　With a Silken Thread.
　The Rebel of the Family.
　"My Love!"

Ione. Three Vols., crown 8vo, 31s. 6d.

Locks and Keys.—On the Development and Distribution of Primitive Locks and Keys. By Lieut.-Gen. PITT-RIVERS, F.R.S. With numerous Illustrations. Demy 4to, half Roxburghe, 16s.

Longfellow :

Longfellow's Complete Prose Works. Including "Outre Mer," "Hyperion," "Kavanagh," "The Poets and Poetry of Europe," and "Driftwood." With Portrait and Illustrations by VALENTINE BROMLEY. Crown 8vo, cloth extra, 7s. 6d.

Longfellow's Poetical Works. Carefully Reprinted from the Original Editions. With numerous fine Illustrations on Steel and Wood. Crown 8vo, cloth extra, 7s. 6d.

Lucy.—Gideon Fleyce: A Novel. By HENRY W. LUCY. Crown 8vo, cloth extra, 3s. 6d.

Lusiad (The) of Camoens. Translated into English Spenserian Verse by ROBERT FFRENCH DUFF. Demy 8vo, with Fourteen full-page Plates, cloth boards, 18s.

McCarthy (Justin, M.P.), Works by :

A History of Our Own Times, from the Accession of Queen Victoria to the General Election of 1880. Four Vols. demy 8vo, cloth extra, 12s. each.—Also a POPULAR EDITION, in Four Vols. crown 8vo, cloth extra, 6s. each.

A Short History of Our Own Times. One Volume, crown 8vo, cloth extra, 6s.

History of the Four Georges. Four Vols. demy 8vo, cloth extra, 12s. each. [In preparation.

Crown 8vo, cloth extra, 3s. 6d. each ; post 8vo, illustrated boards, 2s. each.

Dear Lady Disdain.
The Waterdale Neighbours.
My Enemy's Daughter.
A Fair Saxon.
Linley Rochford
Miss Misanthrope.
Donna Quixote.

The Comet of a Season. Crown 8vo, cloth extra, 3s. 6d.

Maid of Athens. With 12 Illustrations by F. BARNARD. 3 vols., crown 8vo, 31s. 6d.

McCarthy (Justin H.), Works by :

Serapion, and other Poems. Crown 8vo, cloth extra, 6s.

An Outline of the History of Ireland, from the Earliest Times to the Present Day. Cr. 8vo, 1s. ; cloth, 1s. 6d.

MacDonald (George, LL.D.), Works by :

The Princess and Curdie. With 11 Illustrations by JAMES ALLEN. Small crown8 vo, cloth extra, 5s.

Gutta-Percha Willie, the Working Genius. With 9 Illustrations by ARTHUR HUGHES. Square 8vo, cloth extra, 3s. 6d.

Paul Faber, Surgeon. With a Frontispiece by J. E. MILLAIS. Crown 8vo, cloth extra, 3s. 6d.; post 8vo, illustrated boards, 2s.

Thomas Wingfold, Curate. With a Frontispiece by C. J. STANILAND. Crown 8vo, cloth extra, 3s. 6d.; post 8vo, illustrated boards, 2s.

Macdonell.—Quaker Cousins: A Novel. By AGNES MACDONELL. Crown 8vo, cloth extra. 3s. 6d.; post 8vo, illustrated boards, 2s.

Macgregor. — Pastimes and Players. Notes on Popular Games. By ROBERT MACGREGOR. Post 8vo, cloth limp, 2s. 6d.

Maclise Portrait-Gallery (The) of Illustrious Literary Characters; with Memoirs—Biographical, Critical, Bibliographical, and Anecdotal—illustrative of the Literature of the former half of the Present Century. By WILLIAM BATES, B.A. With 85 Portraits printed on an India Tint. Crown 8vo, cloth extra, 7s. 6d.

Macquoid (Mrs.), Works by :

In the Ardennes. With 50 fine Illustrations by THOMAS R. MACQUOID. Square 8vo, cloth extra, 10s. 6d.

Pictures and Legends from Normandy and Brittany. With numerous Illustrations by THOMAS R. MACQUOID. Square 8vo, cloth gilt, 10s. 6d.

Through Normandy. With 90 Illustrations by T. R. MACQUOID. Square 8vo, cloth extra, 7s. 6d.

Through Brittany. With numerous Illustrations by T. R. MACQUOID. Square 8vo, cloth extra, 7s. 6d.

About Yorkshire With 67 Illustrations by T. R. MACQUOID, Engraved by SWAIN. Square 8vo, cloth extra, 10s. 6d.

The Evil Eye, and other Stories. Crown 8vo, cloth extra, 3s. 6d.; post 8vo, illustrated boards, 2s.

Lost Rose, and other Stories. Crown 8vo, cloth extra, 3s. 6d.; post 8vo, illustrated boards, 2s.

**Mackay.—Interludes and Un-
dertones**: or, Music at Twilight. By
CHARLES MACKAY, LL.D. Crown 8vo,
cloth extra, 6s.

Magician's Own Book (The):
Performances with Cups and Balls,
Eggs, Hats, Handkerchiefs, &c. All
from actual Experience. Edited by
W. H. CREMER. With 200 Illustrations.
Crown 8vo, cloth extra, 4s. 6d.

Magic No Mystery : Tricks with
Cards, Dice, Balls, &c., with fully
descriptive Directions; the Art of
Secret Writing ; Training of Perform-
ing Animals, &c. With Coloured
Frontispiece and many Illustrations.
Crown 8vo, cloth extra, 4s. 6d.

Magna Charta. An exact Facsimile of the Original in the British
Museum, printed on fine plate paper,
3 feet by 2 feet, with Arms and Seals
emblazoned in Gold and Colours.
Price 5s.

Mallock (W. H.), Works by :
The New Republic; or, Culture, Faith
and Philosophy in an English Country
House. Post 8vo, cloth limp, 2s. 6d. ;
Cheap Edition, illustrated boards, 2s.

The New Paul and Virginia ; or, Posi-
tivism on an Island. Post 8vo, cloth
limp, 2s. 6d.

Poems. Small 4to, bound in parchment, 8s.

Is Life worth Living? Crown 8vo,
cloth extra, 6s.

Mallory's (Sir Thomas) Mort
d'Arthur : The Stories of King Arthur
and of the Knights of the Round Table.
Edited by B. MONTGOMERIE RANKING.
Post 8vo, cloth limp, 2s.

Marlowe's Works. Including
his Translations. Edited, with Notes
and Introduction, by Col. CUNNING-
HAM. Crown 8vo, cloth extra, 6s.

Marryat (Florence), Novels by:
Crown 8vo, cloth extra, 3s. 6d. each ; or,
post 8vo, illustrated boards, 2s.
Open! Sesame!
Written in Fire.

Post 8vo, illustrated boards, 2s each.
A Harvest of Wild Oats.
A Little Stepson.
Fighting the Air.

Mark Twain, Works by: ɔ
The Choice Works of Mark Twain.
Revised and Corrected throughout by
the Author. With Life, Portrait, and
numerous Illustrations. Crown 8vo,
cloth extra, 7s. 6d.

The Adventures of Tom Sawyer.
With 100 Illustrations. Small 8vo,
cloth extra, 7s. 6d. CHEAP EDITION,
illustrated boards, 2s.

An Idle Excursion, and other Sketches.
Post 8vo, illustrated boards, 2s.

The Prince and the Pauper. With
nearly 200 Illustrations. Crown 8vo,
cloth extra, 7s. 6d.

The Innocents Abroad; or, The New
Pilgrim's Progress : Being some Account of the Steamship " Quaker
City's " Pleasure Excursion to
Europe and the Holy Land. With
234 Illustrations. Crown 8vo, cloth
extra, 7s. 6d. CHEAP EDITION (under
the title of " MARK TWAIN'S PLEASURE
TRIP "), post 8vo, illust. boards, 2s.

A Tramp Abroad. With 314 Illustrations. Crown 8vo, cloth extra, 7s. 6d.

The Stolen White Elephant, &c.
Crown 8vo, cloth extra, 6s.

Life on the Mississippi. With about
300 Original Illustrations. Crown
8vo, cloth extra, 7s. 6d.   .

Massinger's Plays. From the
Text of WILLIAM GIFFORD. Edited
by Col. CUNNINGHAM. Crown 8vo,
cloth extra, 6s.

Mayhew.—London Characters
and the Humorous Side of London
Life. By HENRY MAYHEW. With
numerous Illustrations. Crown 8vo,
cloth extra, 3s. 6d.

Mayfair Library, The :
Post 8vo, cloth limp, 2s. 6d. per Volume
A Journey Round My Room. By
XAVIER DE MAISTRE. Translated
by HENRY ATTWELL.

Latter-Day Lyrics. Edited by W.
DAVENPORT ADAMS.

Quips and Quiddities. Selected by
W. DAVENPORT ADAMS.

The Agony Column of "The Times,"
from 1800 to 1870. Edited, with an
Introduction, by ALICE CLAY.

Balzac's "Comedie Humaine" and
its Author. With Translations by
H. H. WALKER.

Melancholy Anatomised: A Popular
Abridgment of "Burton's Anatomy
of Melancholy."

Gastronomy as a Fine Art. By
BRILLAT-SAVARIN.

MAYFAIR LIBRARY, *continued—*

The Speeches of Charles Dickens. Literary Frivolities, Fancies, Follies, and Frolics. By W. T. DOBSON.

Poetical Ingenuities and Eccentricities. Selected and Edited by W. T. DOBSON.

The Cupboard Papers. By FIN-BEC.

Original Plays by W. S. GILBERT. FIRST SERIES. Containing: The Wicked World — Pygmalion and Galatea— Charity — The Princess— The Palace of Truth—Trial by Jury.

Original Plays by W. S. GILBERT. SECOND SERIES. Containing: Broken Hearts — Engaged — Sweethearts— Gretchen—Dan'l Druce—Tom Cobb —H.M.S. Pinafore — The Sorcerer —The Pirates of Penzance.

Songs of Irish Wit and Humour. Collected and Edited by A. PERCEVAL GRAVES.

Animals and their Masters. By Sir ARTHUR HELPS.

Social Pressure. By Sir ARTHUR HELPS.

Curiosities of Criticism. By HENRY J. JENNINGS.

The Autocrat of the Breakfast-Table. By OLIVER WENDELL HOLMES. Illustrated by J. GORDON THOMSON.

Pencil and Palette. By ROBERT KEMPT.

Little Essays: Passages from the Letters of CHARLES LAMB. Selected and Edited by PERCY FITZGERALD.

Clerical Anecdotes. By JACOB LARWOOD.

Forensic Anecdotes; or, Humour and Curiosities of the Law and Men of Law. By JACOB LARWOOD.

Theatrical Anecdotes. By JACOB LARWOOD.

Carols of Cockayne. By HENRY S. LEIGH.

Jeux d'Esprit. Edited by HENRY S. LEIGH.

True History of Joshua Davidson. By E. LYNN LINTON.

Witch Stories. By E. LYNN LINTON.

Pastimes and Players. By ROBERT MACGREGOR.

The New Paul and Virginia. By W. H. MALLOCK.

The New Republic. By W. H. MALLOCK.

Puck on Pegasus. By H. CHOLMONDELEY-PENNELL.

Pegasus Re-Saddled. By H. CHOLMONDELEY-PENNELL. Illustrated by GEORGE DU MAURIER.

MAYFAIR LIBRARY, *continued—*

Muses of Mayfair. Edited by H. CHOLMONDELEY-PENNELL.

Thoreau: His Life and Aims. By H. A. PAGE.

Puniana. By the Hon. HUGH ROWLEY.

More Puniana. By the Hon. HUGH ROWLEY.

The Philosophy of Handwriting. By DON FELIX DE SALAMANCA.

By Stream and Sea. By WILLIAM SENIOR.

Old Stories Re-told. By WALTER THORNBURY.

Leaves from a Naturalist's Note-Book. By Dr. ANDREW WILSON.

Medicine, Family.—One Thousand Medical Maxims and Surgical Hints, for Infancy, Adult Life, Middle Age, and Old Age. By N. E. DAVIES, Licentiate of the Royal College of Physicians of London. Crown 8vo, 1s. ; cloth, 1s. 6d.

Merry Circle (The): A Book of New Intellectual Games and Amusements. By CLARA BELLEW. With numerous Illustrations. Crown 8vo, cloth extra, 4s. 6d.

Middlemass (Jean), Novels by:

Touch and Go. Crown 8vo, cloth extra, 3s. 6d. ; post 8vo, illustrated boards, 2s.

Mr. Dorillion. Post 8vo, illustrated boards, 2s.

Miller.— Physiology for the Young; or, The House of Life: Human Physiology, with its application to the Preservation of Health. For use in Classes and Popular Reading. With numerous Illustrations. By Mrs. F. FENWICK MILLER. Small 8vo, cloth limp, 2s. 6d.

Milton (J. L.), Works by:

The Hygiene of the Skin. A Concise Set of Rules for the Management of the Skin; with Directions for Diet, Wines, Soaps, Baths, &c. Small 8vo, 1s. ; cloth extra, 1s. 6d.

The Bath in Diseases of the Skin. Small 8vo, 1s. ; cloth extra, 1s. 6d.

The Laws of Life, and their Relation to Diseases of the Skin. Small 8vo, 1s. ; cloth extra, 1s. 6d.

Moncrieff.— The Abdication; or, Time Tries All. An Historical Drama. By W. D. SCOTT-MONCRIEFF. With Seven Etchings by JOHN PETTIE, R.A., W. Q. ORCHARDSON, R.A., J. MACWHIRTER, A.R.A., COLIN HUNTER, R. MACBETH, and TOM GRAHAM. Large 4to, bound in buckram, 21s.

Murray (D. Christie), Novels by. Crown 8vo, cloth extra, 3s. 6d. each; post 8vo, illustrated bds., 2s. each.
A Life's Atonement.
A Model Father.

Crown 8vo, cloth extra, 3s. 6d. each.
Joseph's Coat. With Illustrations by F. BARNARD.
Coals of Fire. With Illustrations by ARTHUR HOPKINS and others.
Val Strange: A Story of the Primrose Way.
Hearts.
By the Gate of the Sea. Illustrated by WILLIAM SMALL.

The Way of the World. Three Vols., crown 8vo, 31s. 6d. [*Shortly*.

North Italian Folk. By Mrs. COMYNS CARR. Illust. by RANDOLPH CALDECOTT. Sq. 8vo, cloth extra, 7s. 6d.

Number Nip (Stories about), the Spirit of the Giant Mountains. Retold for Children by WALTER GRAHAME. With Illustrations by J. MOYR SMITH. Post 8vo, cloth extra, 5s.

Nursery Hints: A Mother's Guide in Health and Disease. By N. E. DAVIES, L.R.C.P. Crown 8vo, 1s.; cloth, 1s. 6d.

Oliphant. — Whiteladies: A Novel. With Illustrations by ARTHUR HOPKINS and HENRY WOODS. Crown 8vo, cloth extra, 3s. 6d.; post 8vo, illustrated boards, 2s.

O'Reilly.—Phœbe's Fortunes: A Novel. With Illustrations by HENRY TUCK. Post 8vo, illustrated boards, 2s.

O'Shaughnessy (Arth.), Works by:
Songs of a Worker. Fcap. 8vo, cloth extra, 7s. 6d.
Music and Moonlight. Fcap. 8vo, cloth extra, 7s. 6d.
Lays of France. Crown 8vo, cloth extra, 10s. 6d.

Ouida, Novels by. Crown 8vo, cloth extra, 5s. each; post 8vo, illustrated boards, 2s. each.
Held in Bondage.
Strathmore.
Chandos.
Under Two Flags.
Cecil Castlemaine's Gage.
Idalia.

OUIDA'S NOVELS, *continued*—
Tricotrin.
Puck.
Folle Farine.
A Dog of Flanders.
Two Little Wooden Shoes.
Pascarel.
Signa.
In a Winter City.
Ariadne.
Friendship.
Moths.
Pipistrello.
A Village Commune.

In Maremma. Crown 8vo, cloth extra, 5s.
Bimbi: Stories for Children. Square 8vo, cloth gilt, cinnamon edges, 7s. 6d.; Popular Edition, crown 8vo, cloth extra, 5s.
Wanda: A Novel. Crown 8vo, cloth extra, 5s.
Wisdom, Wit, and Pathos. Selected from the Works of OUIDA by F. SYDNEY MORRIS. Small crown 8vo, cloth extra, 5s.
Frescoes: Dramatic Sketches. Crown 8vo, cloth extra, 10s. 6d.

Page (H. A.), Works by:
Thoreau: His Life and Aims: A Study. With a Portrait. Post 8vo, cloth limp, 2s. 6d.
Lights on the Way: Some Tales within a Tale. By the late J. H. ALEXANDER, B.A. Edited by H. A. PAGE. Crown 8vo, cloth extra, 6s.

Pascal's Provincial Letters. A New Translation, with Historical Introduction and Notes, by T. M'CRIE, D.D. Post 8vo, cloth limp, 2s.

Paul Ferroll.
Post 8vo, illustrated boards, 2s. each.
Paul Ferroll: A Novel.
Why Paul Ferroll Killed His Wife.

Paul.—Gentle and Simple. By MARGARET AGNES PAUL. With a Frontispiece by HELEN PATERSON. Cr. 8vo, cloth extra, 3s. 6d.; post 8vo, illustrated boards, 2s.

Payn (James), Novels by. Each crown 8vo, cloth extra, 3s. 6d.; or, post 8vo, illustrated boards, 2s.
Lost Sir Massingberd.
The Best of Husbands.
Walter's Word.

JAMES PAYN'S NOVELS, *continued*—
Halves. | Fallen Fortunes.
What He Cost Her.
Less Black than We're Painted
By Proxy
Under One Roof.
High Spirits.
Carlyon's Year.
A Confidential Agent
Some Private Views.
From Exile.

Post 8vo, illustrated boards, 2s. each.
A Perfect Treasure.
Bentinck's Tutor.
Murphy's Master
A County Family.
At Her Mercy.
A Woman's Vengeance
Cecil's Tryst.
The Clyffards of Clyffe.
The Family Scapegrace.
The Foster Brothers.
Found Dead.
Gwendoline's Harvest.
Humorous Stories.
Like Father, Like Son.
A Marine Residence.
Married Beneath Him.
Mirk Abbey.
Not Wooed, but Won.
Two Hundred Pounds Reward.

Crown 8vo, cloth extra, 3s. 6d. each.
A Grape from a Thorn. With Illustrations by W. SMALL.
For Cash Only. | Kit: A Memory.

The Canon's Ward. Three Vols., crown 8vo. [*Shortly.*

Pennell (H. Cholmondeley),
Works by: Post 8vo, cloth limp, 2s. 6d. each.
Puck on Pegasus. With Illustrations.
The Muses of Mayfair. Vers de Société, Selected and Edited by H. C. PENNELL.
Pegasus Re-Saddled. With numerous full-page Illustrations by GEORGE DU MAURIER.

Phelps.—Beyond the Gates.
By ELIZABETH STUART PHELPS, Author of "The Gates Ajar." Crown 8vo, cloth extra, 2s. 6d. Published by special arrangement with the Author, and Copyright in England and its Dependencies.

Planche (J. R.), Works by:
The Cyclopædia of Costume; or, A Dictionary of Dress—Regal, Ecclesiastical, Civil, and Military—from the Earliest Period in England to the Reign of George the Third. Including Notices of Contemporaneous Fashions on the Continent, and a General History of the Costumes of the Principal Countries of Europe. Two Vols., demy 4to, half morocco, profusely Illustrated with Coloured and Plain Plates and Woodcuts, £7 7s. The Vols. may also be had *separately* (each complete in itself) at £3 13s. 6d. each: Vol. I. THE DICTIONARY. Vol. II. A GENERAL HISTORY OF COSTUME IN EUROPE.

The Pursuivant of Arms; or, Heraldry Founded upon Facts. With Coloured Frontispiece and 200 Illustrations. Crown 8vo, cloth extra, 7s. 6d.

Songs and Poems, from 1819 to 1879. Edited, with an Introduction, by his Daughter, Mrs. MACKARNESS. Crown 8vo, cloth extra, 6s.

Pirkis.—Trooping with Crows:
A Story. By CATHERINE PIRKIS. Fcap. 8vo, picture cover, 1s.

Play-time : Sayings and Doings of Babyland. By EDWARD STANFORD. Large 4to, handsomely printed in Colours, 5s.

Plutarch's Lives of Illustrious Men. Translated from the Greek, with Notes Critical and Historical, and a Life of Plutarch, by JOHN and WILLIAM LANGHORNE. Two Vols., 8vo, cloth extra, with Portraits, 10s. 6d.

Poe (Edgar Allan):—
The Choice Works, in Prose and Poetry, of EDGAR ALLAN POE. With an Introductory Essay by CHARLES BAUDELAIRE, Portrait and Facsimiles. Crown 8vo, cloth extra, 7s. 6d.

The Mystery of Marie Roget, and other Stories. Post 8vo, illustrated boards, 2s.

Pope's Poetical Works. Complete in One Volume. Post 8vo, cloth limp, 2s.

Price (E. C.), Novels by:
Valentina: A Sketch. With a Frontispiece by HAL LUDLOW. Crown 8vo, cloth extra, 3s. 6d.; post 8vo, illustrated boards, 2s.

The Foreigners. Three Vols., crown 8vo, 31s. 6d.

Proctor (Richd. A.), Works by:

Flowers of the Sky. With 55 Illustrations. Small crown 8vo, cloth extra, 4s. 6d.

Easy Star Lessons. With Star Maps for Every Night in the Year, Drawings of the Constellations, &c. Crown 8vo, cloth extra, 6s.

Familiar Science Studies. Crown 8vo, cloth extra, 7s. 6d.

Rough Ways made Smooth: A Series of Familiar Essays on Scientific Subjects. Cr. 8vo, cloth extra, 6s.

Our Place among Infinities: A Series of Essays contrasting our Little Abode in Space and Time with the Infinities Around us. Crown 8vo, cloth extra, 6s.

The Expanse of Heaven: A Series of Essays on the Wonders of the Firmament. Cr. 8vo, cloth extra, 6s.

Saturn and its System. New and Revised Edition, with 13 Steel Plates. Demy 8vo, cloth extra, 10s. 6d.

The Great Pyramid: Observatory, Tomb, and Temple. With Illustrations. Crown 8vo, cloth extra, 6s.

Mysteries of Time and Space. With Illustrations. Crown 8vo, cloth extra, 7s. 6d.

Wages and Wants of Science Workers. Crown 8vo, 1s. 6d.

Pyrotechnist's Treasury (The); or, Complete Art of Making Fireworks. By THOMAS KENTISH. With numerous Illustrations. Crown 8vo, cloth extra, 4s. 6d.

Rabelais' Works. Faithfully Translated from the French, with variorum Notes, and numerous characteristic Illustrations by GUSTAVE DORÉ. Crown 8vo, cloth extra, 7s. 6d.

Rambosson.—Popular Astronomy. By J. RAMBOSSON, Laureate of the Institute of France. Translated by C. B. PITMAN. Crown 8vo, cloth gilt, with numerous Illustrations, and a beautifully executed Chart of Spectra, 7s. 6d.

Reader's Handbook (The) of Allusions, References, Plots, and Stories. By the Rev. Dr. BREWER. Third Edition, revised throughout, with a New Appendix, containing a COMPLETE ENGLISH BIBLIOGRAPHY. Crown 8vo, 1,400 pages, cloth extra, 7s. 6d.

Reade (Charles, D.C.L.), Novels by. Each post 8vo, illustrated boards, 2s.; or crown 8vo, cloth extra, illustrated, 3s. 6d.

Peg Woffington. Illustrated by S. L. FILDES, A.R.A.

Christie Johnstone. Illustrated by WILLIAM SMALL.

It is Never Too Late to Mend. Illustrated by G. J. PINWELL.

The Course of True Love Never did run Smooth. Illustrated by HELEN PATERSON.

The Autobiography of a Thief; Jack of all Trades; and James Lambert. Illustrated by MATT STRETCH.

Love me Little, Love me Long. Illustrated by M. ELLEN EDWARDS.

The Double Marriage. Illustrated by Sir JOHN GILBERT, R.A., and CHARLES KEENE.

The Cloister and the Hearth. Illustrated by CHARLES KEENE.

Hard Cash. Illustrated by F. W. LAWSON.

Griffith Gaunt. Illustrated by S. L. FILDES, A.R.A., and WM. SMALL.

Foul Play. Illustrated by GEORGE DU MAURIER.

Put Yourself in His Place. Illustrated by ROBERT BARNES.

A Terrible Temptation. Illustrated by EDWARD HUGHES and A. W. COOPER.

The Wandering Heir. Illustrated by HELEN PATERSON, S. L. FILDES, A.R.A., CHARLES GREEN, and HENRY WOODS, A.R.A.

A Simpleton. Illustrated by KATE CRAUFORD.

A Woman-Hater. Illustrated by THOS. COULDERY.

Readiana. With a Steel Plate Portrait of CHARLES READE.

A New Collection of Stories. In Three Vols., crown 8vo. [*Preparing.*

Richardson. — A Ministry of Health, and other Papers. By BENJAMIN WARD RICHARDSON, M.D., &c. Crown 8vo, cloth extra, 6s.

Riddell (Mrs. J. H.), Novels by:

Her Mother's Darling. Crown 8vo, cloth extra, 3s. 6d.; post 8vo, illustrated boards, 2s.

The Prince of Wales's Garden Party, and other Stories. With a Frontispiece by M. ELLEN EDWARDS. Crown 8vo, cloth extra, 3s. 6d.

Rimmer (Alfred), Works by:
Our Old Country Towns. By ALFRED RIMMER. With over 50 Illustrations by the Author. Square 8vo, cloth extra, gilt, 10s. 6d.

Rambles Round Eton and Harrow. By ALFRED RIMMER. With 50 Illustrations by the Author. Square 8vo, cloth gilt, 10s. 6d.

About England with Dickens. With 58 Illustrations by ALFRED RIMMER and C. A. VANDERHOOF. Square 8vo, cloth gilt, 10s. 6d.

Robinson (F. W.), Novels by:
Women are Strange. Crown 8vo, cloth extra, 3s. 6d.

The Hands of Justice. Crown 8vo, cloth extra, 3s. 6d.

Robinson (Phil), Works by:
The Poets' Birds. Crown 8vo, cloth extra, 7s. 6d.

The Poets' Beasts. Crown 8vo, cloth extra, 7s. 6d.   [*In preparation.*]

Robinson Crusoe: A beautiful reproduction of Major's Edition, with 37 Woodcuts and Two Steel Plates by GEORGE CRUIKSHANK, choicely printed. Crown 8vo, cloth extra, 7s. 6d. 100 ● Large-Paper copies, printed on handmade paper, with India proofs of the Illustrations, price 36s.

Rochefoucauld's Maxims and Moral Reflections. With Notes, and an Introductory Essay by SAINTE-BEUVE. Post 8vo, cloth limp, 2s.

Roll of Battle Abbey, The; or, A List of the Principal Warriors who came over from Normandy with William the Conqueror, and Settled in this Country, A.D. 1066-7. With the principal Arms emblazoned in Gold and Colours. Handsomely printed, price 5s.

Rowley (Hon. Hugh), Works by:
Post 8vo, cloth limp, 2s. 6d. each.

Puniana: Riddles and Jokes. With numerous Illustrations.

More Puniana. Profusely Illustrated.

Russell (Clark).—Round the Galley-Fire. By W. CLARK RUSSELL, Author of "The Wreck of the *Grosvenor.*" Cr. 8vo, cloth extra, 6s.

Sala.—Gaslight and Daylight. By GEORGE AUGUSTUS SALA. Post 8vo, illustrated boards, 2s.

Sanson.—Seven Generations of Executioners: Memoirs of the Sanson Family (1688 to 1847). Edited by HENRY SANSON. Crown 8vo, cloth extra, 3s. 6d.

Saunders (John), Novels by:
Crown 8vo, cloth extra, 3s. 6d. each; or post 8vo, illustrated boards, 2s. each.

Bound to the Wheel.

One Against the World.

Guy Waterman

The Lion in the Path.

The Two Dreamers.

Science Gossip: An Illustrated Medium of Interchange and Gossip for Students and Lovers of Nature. Edited by J. E. TAYLOR, Ph.D., F.L.S., F.G.S. Monthly, price 4d; Annual Subscription 5s. (including Postage). Vols. I. to XIV. may be had at 7s. 6d. each; and Vols. XV. to XIX. (1883), at 5s. each. Among the subjects included in its pages will be found: Aquaria, Bees, Beetles, Birds, Butterflies, Ferns, Fish, Flies, Fossils, Fungi, Geology, Lichens, Microscopes, Mosses, Moths, Reptiles, Seaweeds, Spiders, Telescopes, Wild Flowers, Worms, &c.

"Secret Out" Series, The:
Crown 8vo, cloth extra, profusely Illustrated, 4s. 6d. each.

The Secret Out: One Thousand Tricks with Cards, and other Recreations; with Entertaining Experiments in Drawing-room or "White Magic." By W. H. CREMER. 300 Engravings.

The Pyrotechnist's Treasury; or, Complete Art of Making Fireworks. By THOMAS KENTISH. With numerous Illustrations.

The Art of Amusing: A Collection of Graceful Arts, Games, Tricks, Puzzles, and Charades. By FRANK BELLEW. With 300 Illustrations.

Hanky-Panky: Very Easy Tricks, Very Difficult Tricks, White Magic, Sleight of Hand. Edited by W. H. CREMER. With 200 Illustrations.

The Merry Circle: A Book of New Intellectual Games and Amusements. By CLARA BELLEW. With many Illustrations.

Magician's Own Book: Performances with Cups and Balls, Eggs, Hats, Handkerchiefs, &c. All from actual Experience. Edited by W. H. CREMER. 200 Illustrations.

THE "SECRET OUT" SERIES, *continued*—
Magic No Mystery: Tricks with Cards, Dice, Balls, &c., with fully descriptive Directions; the Art of Secret Writing; Training of Performing Animals, &c. With Coloured Frontispiece and many Illustrations.

Senior (William), Works by :

Travel and Trout in the Antipodes. Crown 8vo, cloth extra, 6s.

By Stream and Sea. Post 8vo, cloth limp, 2s. 6d.

Seven Sagas (The) of Prehistoric Man. By JAMES H. STODDART,
Author of "The Village Life." Crown 8vo, cloth extra, 6s.   [*Shortly.*

Shakespeare :

The First Folio Shakespeare.—MR. WILLIAM SHAKESPEARE's Comedies, Histories, and Tragedies. Published according to the true Originall Copies. London, Printed by ISAAC IAGGARD and ED. BLOUNT. 1623.—A Reproduction of the extremely rare original, in reduced facsimile, by a photographic process—ensuring the strictest accuracy in every detail. Small 8vo, half-Roxburghe, 7s. 6d.

The Lansdowne Shakespeare. Beautifully printed in red and black, in small but very clear type. With engraved facsimile of DROESHOUT's Portrait. Post 8vo, cloth extra, 7s. 6d.

Shakespeare for Children: Tales from Shakespeare. By CHARLES and MARY LAMB. With numerous Illustrations, coloured and plain, by J. MOYR SMITH. Crown 4to, cloth gilt, 6s.

The Handbook of Shakespeare Music. Being an Account of 350 Pieces of Music, set to Words taken from the Plays and Poems of Shakespeare, the compositions ranging from the Elizabethan Age to the Present Time. By ALFRED ROFFE. 4to, half-Roxburghe, 7s.

A Study of Shakespeare. By ALGERNON CHARLES SWINBURNE. Crown 8vo, cloth extra, 8s.

Shelley's Complete Works, in
Four Vols., post 8vo, cloth limp, 8s.; or separately, 2s. each. Vol. I. contains his Early Poems, Queen Mab, &c., with an Introduction by LEIGH HUNT; Vol. II., his Later Poems, Laon and Cythna, &c.; Vol. III., Posthumous Poems, the Shelley Papers, &c.; Vol. IV., his Prose Works, including A Refutation of Deism, Zastrozzi, St. Irvyne, &c.

Sheridan's Complete Works,
with Life and Anecdotes. Including his Dramatic Writings, printed from the Original Editions, his Works in Prose and Poetry, Translations, Speeches, Jokes, Puns, &c. With a Collection of Sheridaniana. Crown 8vo, cloth extra, gilt, with 10 full-page Tinted Illustrations, 7s. 6d.

Short Sayings of Great Men.
With Historical and Explanatory Notes by SAMUEL A. BENT, M.A. Demy 8vo, cloth extra, 7s. 6d.

Sidney's (Sir Philip) Complete
Poetical Works, including all those in "Arcadia." With Portrait, Memorial-Introduction, Essay on the Poetry of Sidney, and Notes, by the Rev. A. B. GROSART, D.D. Three Vols., crown 8vo, cloth boards, 18s.

Signboards: Their History.
With Anecdotes of Famous Taverns and Remarkable Characters. By JACOB LARWOOD and JOHN CAMDEN HOTTEN. Crown 8vo, cloth extra, with 100 Illustrations, 7s. 6d.

Sims (G. R.).—How the Poor
Live. By GEORGE R. SIMS. With 60 Illustrations by FREDERICK BARNARD. Large 4to, 1s.   ●

Sketchley.—A Match in the
Dark. By ARTHUR SKETCHLEY. Post 8vo, illustrated boards, 2s.

Slang Dictionary, The: Etymological, Historical, and Anecdotal.
Crown 8vo, cloth extra, gilt, 6s. 6d.

Smith (J. Moyr), Works by :

The Prince of Argolis: A Story of the Old Greek Fairy Time. By J. MOYR SMITH. Small 8vo, cloth extra, with 130 Illustrations, 3s. 6d.

Tales of Old Thule. Collected and Illustrated by J. MOYR SMITH. Crown 8vo, cloth gilt, profusely Illustrated, 6s.

The Wooing of the Water Witch: A Northern Oddity. By EVAN DALDORNE. Illustrated by J. MOYR SMITH. Small 8vo, cloth extra, 6s.

South-West, The New : Travelling Sketches from Kansas, New
Mexico, Arizona, and Northern Mexico. By ERNST VON HESSE-WARTEGG. With 100 fine Illustrations and 3 Maps. 8vo, cloth extra, 14s. [*In preparation.*

Spalding.–Elizabethan Demon-ology: An Essay in Illustration of the Belief in the Existence of Devils, and the Powers possessed by Them. By T. ALFRED SPALDING, LL.B. Crown 8vo, cloth extra, 5s.

Speight. — The Mysteries of Heron Dyke. By T. W. SPEIGHT. With a Frontispiece by M. ELLEN EDWARDS. Crown 8vo, cloth extra, 3s. 6d.; post 8vo, illustrated boards, 2s.

Spenser for Children. By M. H. TOWRY. With Illustrations by WALTER J. MORGAN. Crown 4to, with Coloured Illustrations, cloth gilt, 6s.

Staunton.—Laws and Practice of Chess; Together with an Analysis of the Openings, and a Treatise on End Games. By HOWARD STAUNTON. Edited by ROBERT B. WORMALD. A New Edition, small crown 8vo, cloth extra, 5s.

Stedman. — Victorian Poets: Critical Essays. By EDMUND CLARENCE STEDMAN. Crown 8vo, extra, 9s.

Sterndale.—The Afghan Knife: A Novel. By ROBERT ARMITAGE STERN-DALE. Cr. 8vo, cloth extra, 3s. 6d.; post 8vo, illustrated boards, 2s.

Stevenson (R.Louis), Works by:
Familiar Studies of Men and Books. Crown 8vo, cloth extra, 6s.
New Arabian Nights. New and Cheaper Edit. Cr.8vo, cloth extra, 6s.
The Silverado Squatters: Sketches from a Californian Mountain. With Frontispiece. Cr.8vo, cloth extra, 6s.

St. John.—A Levantine Family. By BAYLE ST. JOHN. Post 8vo, illustrated boards, 2s.

Stoddard.—Summer Cruising in the South Seas. By CHARLES WARREN STODDARD. Illustrated by WALLIS MACKAY. Crown 8vo, cloth extra, 3s. 6d.

St. Pierre.—Paul and Virginia, and The Indian Cottage. By BER-NARDIN DE ST. PIERRE. Edited, with Life, by the Rev. E. CLARKE. Post 8vo, cloth limp, 2s.

Stories from Foreign Novel-ists. With Notices of their Lives and Writings. By HELEN and ALICE ZIM-MERN; and a Frontispiece. Crown 8vo, cloth extra, 3s. 6d. [Shortly.

Strutt's Sports and Pastimes of the People of England; including the Rural and Domestic Recreations, May Games, Mummeries, Shows, Pro-cessions, Pageants, and Pompous Spectacles, from the Earliest Period to the Present Time. With 140 Illus-trations. Edited by WILLIAM HONE. Crown 8vo, cloth extra, 7s. 6d.

Suburban Homes (The) of London: A Residential Guide to Favourite London Localities, their Society, Celebrities, and Associations. With Notes on their Rental, Rates, and House Accommodation. With a Map of Suburban London. Crown 8vo, cloth extra, 7s. 6d.

Swift's Choice Works, in Prose and Verse. With Memoir, Portrait, and Facsimiles of the Maps in the Original Edition of "Gulliver's Travels." Cr. 8vo, cloth extra, 7s. 6d.

Swinburne (Algernon C.), Works by:
The Queen Mother and Rosamond. Fcap. 8vo, 5s.
Atalanta in Calydon. Crown 8vo, 6s.
Chastelard. A Tragedy. Crown 8vo, 7s.
Poems and Ballads. FIRST SERIES. Fcap. 8vo, 9s. Also in crown 8vo, at same price.
Poems and Ballads. SECOND SERIES. Fcap. 8vo, 9s. Also in crown 8vo, at same price.
Notes on Poems and Reviews. 8vo, 1s.
William Blake: A Critical Essay. With Facsimile Paintings. Demy 8vo, 16s.
Songs before Sunrise. Crown 8vo, 10s. 6d.
Bothwell: A Tragedy. Crown 8vo, 12s. 6d.
George Chapman: An Essay. Crown 8vo, 7s.
Songs of Two Nations. Crown 8vo, 6s.
Essays and Studies. Crown 8vo, 12s.
Erechtheus: A Tragedy. Crown 8vo, 6s.
Note of an English Republican on the Muscovite Crusade. 8vo, 1s.
A Note on Charlotte Bronte. Crown 8vo, 6s.
A Study of Shakespeare. Crown 8vo, 8s.
Songs of the Springtides. Crown 8vo, 6s.

A. C. Swinburne's Works, *continued*—

Studies in Song. Crown 8vo, 7s.

Mary Stuart: A Tragedy. Crown 8vo, 8s.

Tristram of Lyonesse, and other Poems. Crown 8vo, 9s.

A Century of Roundels. Small 4to, cloth extra, 8s.

Syntax's (Dr.) Three Tours: In Search of the Picturesque, in Search of Consolation, and in Search of a Wife. With the whole of Rowland-son's droll page Illustrations in Colours and a Life of the Author by J. C. Hotten. Medium 8vo, cloth extra, 7s. 6d.

Taine's History of English Literature. Translated by Henry Van Laun. Four Vols., small 8vo, cloth boards, 30s.—Popular Edition, in Two Vols., crown 8vo, cloth extra, 15s.

Taylor's (Bayard) Diversions of the Echo Club: Burlesques of Modern Writers. Post 8vo, cloth limp, 2s.

Taylor's (Tom) Historical Dramas: "Clancarty," "Jeanne Darc," "'Twixt Axe and Crown," "The Fool's Revenge," "Arkwright's Wife," "Anne Boleyn," "Plot and Passion." One Vol., crown 8vo, cloth extra, 7s. 6d.

. The Plays may also be had separately, at 1s. each.

Thackerayana: Notes and Anecdotes. Illustrated by Hundreds of Sketches by William Makepeace Thackeray, depicting Humorous Incidents in his School-life, and Favourite Characters in the books of his every-day reading. With Coloured Frontispiece. Crown 8vo, cloth extra, 7s. 6d.

Thomas (Bertha), Novels by. Each crown 8vo, cloth extra, 3s. 6d.; or post 8vo, illustrated boards, 2s.

    Cressida.

    Proud Maisie.

    The Violin-Player.

Thomson's Season and Castle of Indolence. With a Biographical and Critical Introduction by Allan Cunningham, and over 50 fine Illustrations on Steel and Wood. Crown 8vo, cloth extra, gilt edges, 7s. 6d.

Thornbury (Walter), Works by:

Haunted London. Edited by Edward Walford, M.A. With Illustrations by F. W. Fairholt, F.S.A. Crown 8vo, cloth extra, 7s. 6d.

The Life and Correspondence of J. M. W. Turner. Founded upon Letters and Papers furnished by his Friends and fellow Academicians. With numerous Illustrations in Colours, facsimiled from Turner's Original Drawings. Crown 8vo, cloth extra, 7s. 6d.

Old Stories Re-told. Post 8vo, cloth limp, 2s. 6d.

Tales for the Marines. Post 8vo, illustrated boards, 2s.

Timbs (John), Works by:

The History of Clubs and Club Life in London. With Anecdotes of its Famous Coffee-houses, Hostelries, and Taverns. With numerous Illustrations. Cr. 8vo, cloth extra, 7s. 6d.

English Eccentrics and Eccentricities: Stories of Wealth and Fashion, Delusions, Impostures, and Fanatic Missions, Strange Sights and Sporting Scenes, Eccentric Artists, Theatrical Folks, Men of Letters, &c. With nearly 50 Illusts. Crown 8vo, cloth extra, 7s. 6d.

Torrens. — The Marquess Wellesley, Architect of Empire. An Historic Portrait. By W. M. Torrens, M.P. Demy 8vo, cloth extra, 14s.

Trollope (Anthony), Novels by:

The Way We Live Now. With Illustrations. Crown 8vo, cloth extra, 3s. 6d. post 8vo, illust. boards, 2s.

The American Senator. Cr. 8vo, cl. extra, 3s. 6d.; post 8vo, illust. bds., 2s.

Kept in the Dark. With a Frontispiece by J. E. Millais, R.A. Crown 8vo, cloth extra, 3s. 6d.

Frau Frohmann, &c. With Frontispiece. Crown 8vo, cloth extra, 3s. 6d.

Marion Fay. Cr. 8vo, cl. extra, 3s. 6d.

Mr. Scarborough's Family. Crown 8vo, cloth extra, 3s. 6d.

The Land-Leaguers. Three Vols., crown 8vo, 31s. 6d.

Trollope (Frances E.), Works by: Crown 8vo, cloth extra, 3s. 6d. each.

Like Ships upon the Sea.

Mabel's Progress.

Anne Furness.

Trollope (T. A.).—Diamond Cut
Diamond, and other Stories. By
THOMAS ADOLPHUS TROLLOPE. Crown
8vo, cloth extra, 3s. 6d.; post 8vo,
illustrated boards, 2s.

Tytler (Sarah), Novels by:
What She Came Through. Crown
8vo, cloth extra, 3s. 6d.; post 8vo,
illustrated boards, 2s.
The Bride's Pass. With a Frontispiece by P. MACNAB. Crown 8vo,
cloth extra, 3s. 6d.

Van Laun.—History of French
Literature. By HENRY VAN LAUN.
Complete in Three Vols., demy 8vo,
cloth boards, 7s. 6d. each.

Villari. — A Double Bond: A
Story. By LINDA VILLARI. Fcap.
8vo, picture cover, 1s.

Walcott.— Church Work and
Life in English Minsters; and the
English Student's Monasticon. By the
Rev. MACKENZIE E. C. WALCOTT, B.D.
Two Vols., crown 8vo, cloth extra,
with Map and Ground-Plans, 14s.

Walford (Edw., M.A.),Works by:
The County Families of the United
Kingdom. Containing Notices of
the Descent, Birth, Marriage, Educa-
tion, &c., of more than 12,000 dis-
tinguished Heads of Families, their
Heirs Apparent or Presumptive, the
Offices they hold or have held, their
Town and Country Addresses, Clubs,
&c. Twenty-fourth Annual Edition,
for 1884, cloth, full gilt, 50s. [Shortly.
The Shilling Peerage (1883). Con-
taining an Alphabetical List of the
House of Lords, Dates of Creation,
Lists of Scotch and Irish Peers,
Addresses, &c. 32mo, cloth, 1s.
Published annually.
The Shilling Baronetage (1883).
Containing an Alphabetical List of
the Baronets of the United Kingdom,
Short Biographical Notices, Dates
of Creation, Addresses, &c. 32mo,
cloth, 1s. Published annually.
The Shilling Knightage (1883). Containing an Alphabetical List of the
Knights of the United Kingdom,
short Biographical Notices, Dates
of Creation, Addresses, &c. 32mo,
cloth, 1s. Published annually.
The Shilling House of Commons
(1883). Containing a List of all the
Members of the British Parliament,
their Town and Country Addresses,
&c. 32mo, cloth, 1s. Published
annually.

EDW. WALFORD'S WORKS, continued—
The Complete Peerage, Baronetage, Knightage, and House of
Commons (1883). In One Volume,
royal 32mo, cloth extra, gilt edges,
5s. Published annually.
Haunted London. By WALTER
THORNBURY. Edited by EDWARD
WALFORD, M.A. With Illustrations
by F. W. FAIRHOLT, F.S.A. Crown
8vo, cloth extra, 7s. 6d.

Walton and Cotton's Complete
Angler; or, The Contemplative Man's
Recreation; being a Discourse of
Rivers, Fishponds, Fish and Fishing,
written by IZAAK WALTON; and In-
structions how to Angle for a Trout or
Grayling in a clear Stream, by CHARLES
COTTON. With Original Memoirs and
Notes by Sir HARRIS NICOLAS, and
61 Copperplate Illustrations. Large
crown 8vo, cloth antique, 7s. 6d.

Wanderer's Library, The:
Crown 8vo, cloth extra, 3s. 6d. each.
Wanderings in Patagonia; or, Life
among the Ostrich Hunters. By
JULIUS BEERBOHM. Illustrated.
Camp Notes: Stories of Sport and
Adventure in Asia, Africa, and
America. By FREDERICK BOYLE.
Savage Life. By FREDERICK BOYLE.
Merrie England in the Olden Time.
By GEORGE DANIEL. With Illustra-
tions by ROBT. CRUIKSHANK.
Circus Life and Circus Celebrities.
By THOMAS FROST.
The Lives of the Conjurers. By
THOMAS FROST.
The Old Showmen and the Old
London Fairs. By THOMAS FROST.
Low-Life Deeps. An Account of the
Strange Fish to be found there. By
JAMES GREENWOOD.
The Wilds of London. By JAMES
GREENWOOD.
Tunis: The Land and the People.
By the Chevalier de HESSE-WAR-
TEGG. With 22 Illustrations.
The Life and Adventures of a Cheap
Jack. By One of the Fraternity.
Edited by CHARLES HINDLEY.
The World Behind the Scenes. By
PERCY FITZGERALD.
Tavern Anecdotes and Sayings:
Including the Origin of Signs, and
Reminiscences connected with Ta-
verns, Coffee Houses, Clubs, &c.
By CHARLES HINDLEY. With Illusts.
The Genial Showman: Life and Ad-
ventures of Artemus Ward. By E. P.
HINGSTON. With a Frontispiece.

The Wanderer's Library, *continued—*

The Story of the London Parks. By JACOB LARWOOD. With Illusts.

London Characters. By HENRY MAYHEW. Illustrated.

Seven Generations of Executioners: Memoirs of the Sanson Family (1688 to 1847). Edited by HENRY SANSON.

Summer Cruising in the South Seas. By CHARLES WARREN STODDARD. Illust. by WALLIS MACKAY.

Warner.—A Roundabout Journey. By CHARLES DUDLEY WARNER, Author of " My Summer in a Garden." Crown 8vo, cloth extra, 6s.

Warrants, &c. :—

Warrant to Execute Charles I. An exact Facsimile, with the Fifty-nine Signatures, and corresponding Seals. Carefully printed on paper to imitate the Original, 22 in. by 14 in. Price 2s.

Warrant to Execute Mary Queen of Scots. An exact Facsimile, including the Signature of Queen Elizabeth, and a Facsimile of the Great Seal. Beautifully printed on paper to imitate the Original MS. Price 2s.

Magna Charta. An Exact Facsimile of the Original Document in the British Museum, printed on fine plate paper, nearly 3 feet long by 2 feet wide, with the Arms and Seals emblazoned in Gold and Colours. Price 5s.

The Roll of Battle Abbey; or, A List of the Principal Warriors who came over from Normandy with William the Conqueror, and Settled in this Country, A.D. 1066–7. With the principal Arms emblazoned in Gold and Colours. Price 5s.

Westropp.—Handbook of Pottery and Porcelain; or, History of those Arts from the Earliest Period. By HODDER M. WESTROPP. With numerous Illustrations, and a List of Marks. Crown 8vo, cloth limp, 4s. 6d.

Whistler v. Ruskin: Art and Art Critics. By J. A. MACNEILL WHISTLER. Seventh Edition, square 8vo, 1s.

White's Natural History of Selborne. Edited, with Additions, by THOMAS BROWN, F.L.S. Post 8vo, cloth limp, 2s.

Wilson (Dr. Andrew, F.R.S.E.), Works by:

Chapters on Evolution: A Popular History of the Darwinian and Allied Theories of Development. Second Edition. Crown 8vo, cloth extra, with 259 Illustrations, 7s. 6d.

Leaves from a Naturalist's Notebook. Post 8vo, cloth limp, 2s. 6d.

Leisure-Time Studies, chiefly Biological. Second Edition. Crown 8vo, cloth extra, with Illustrations, 6s.

Williams (W. Mattieu, F.R.A.S.), Works by:

Science in Short Chapters. Crown 8vo, cloth extra, 7s. 6d.

A Simple Treatise on Heat. Crown 8vo, cloth limp, with Illustrations, 2s. 6d.

Wilson (C. E.).—Persian Wit and Humour: Being the Sixth Book of the Baharistan of Jami, Translated for the first time from the Original Persian into English Prose and Verse. With Notes by C. E. WILSON, M.R.A.S., Assistant Librarian Royal Academy of Arts. Cr. 8vo, parchment binding, 4s.

Winter (J. S.), Stories by :

Cavalry Life. Crown 8vo, cloth extra, 3s. 6d.

Regimental Legends. Crown 8vo, cloth extra, 3s. 6d.

Wood.—Sabina: A Novel. By Lady WOOD. Post 8vo, illustrated boards, 2s.

Words, Facts, and Phrases : A Dictionary of Curious, Quaint, and Out-of-the-Way Matters. By ELIEZER EDWARDS. Crown 8vo, half-bound, 12s. 6d.

Wright (Thomas), Works by :

Caricature History of the Georges. (The House of Hanover.) With 400 Pictures, Caricatures, Squibs, Broadsides, Window Pictures, &c. Crown 8vo, cloth extra, 7s. 6d.

History of Caricature and of the Grotesque in Art, Literature, Sculpture, and Painting. Profusely Illustrated by F. W. FAIRHOLT, F.S.A. Large post 8vo, cloth extra, 7s. 6d.

Yates (Edmund), Novels by :

Post 8vo, illustrated boards 2s. each.

Castaway.

The Forlorn Hope.

Land at Last.

NOVELS BY THE BEST AUTHORS.

NEW NOVELS at every Library.

All In a Garden Fair. By WALTER BESANT. Three Vols.

Annan Water. By ROBERT BUCHANAN. Three Vols.

Fancy-Free, &c. By CHARLES GIBBON. Three Vols. • [Shortly.

Fortune's Fool. By JULIAN HAW-THORNE. Three Vols.

Beatrix Randolph. By JULIAN HAW-THORNE. Two Vols. [Shortly.

Ione. E. LYNN LINTON. Three Vols.

The Way of the World. By D. CHRIS-TIE MURRAY. Three Vols. [Shortly.

The Foreigners. By E. C. PRICE. Three Vols.

Maid of Athens. By JUSTIN McCARTHY, M.P. With 12 Illustrations by FRED. BARNARD. Three Vols.

The Canon's Ward. By JAMES PAYN. Three Vols. [Shortly.

A New Collection of Stories by CHARLES READE. Three Vols. [Shortly.

The Land-Leaguers. By ANTHONY TROLLOPE. Three Vols.

THE PICCADILLY NOVELS.

Popular Stories by the Best Authors. LIBRARY EDITIONS, many Illustrated, crown 8vo, cloth extra, 3s. 6d. each.

BY MRS. ALEXANDER.
Maid, Wife, or Widow?

BY W. BESANT & JAMES RICE.
Ready-Money Mortiboy
My Little Girl
The Case of Mr. Lucraft.
This Son of Vulcan.
With Harp and Crown.
The Golden Butterfly.
By Celia's Arbour.
The Monks of Thelema.
'Twas In Trafalgar's Bay.
The Seamy Side.
The Ten Years' Tenant.
The Chaplain of the Fleet.

BY WALTER BESANT.
All Sorts and Conditions of Men.
The Captains' Room.

BY ROBERT BUCHANAN.
A Child of Nature.
God and the Man.
The Shadow of the Sword.
The Martyrdom of Madeline
Love Me for Ever.

BY MRS. H. LOVETT CAMERON.
Deceivers Ever.
Juliet's Guardian.

BY MORTIMER COLLINS.
Sweet Anne Page.
Transmigration.
From Midnight to Midnight.

MORTIMER & FRANCES COLLINS.
Blacksmith and Scholar.
The Village Comedy.
You Play me False.

BY WILKIE COLLINS.

Antonina.	New Magdalen.
Basil.	The Frozen Deep.
Hide and Seek.	The Law and the
The Dead Secret.	Lady.
Queen of Hearts.	The Two Destinies
My Miscellanies.	Haunted Hotel
Woman in White.	The Fallen Leaves
The Moonstone.	Jezebel's Daughter
Man and Wife.	The Black Robe.
Poor Miss Finch.	Heart and Science
Miss or Mrs?	

BY DUTTON COOK.
Paul Foster's Daughter.

BY WILLIAM CYPLES.
Hearts of Gold.

BY JAMES DE MILLE.
A Castle In Spain.

BY J. LEITH DERWENT.
Our Lady of Tears. | Circe's Lovers.

PICCADILLY NOVELS, *continued*—

BY M. BETHAM-EDWARDS.
Felicia. | Kitty.

BY MRS. ANNIE EDWARDES.
Archie Lovell.

BY R. E. FRANCILLON.
Olympia. | Queen Cophetua.
One by One.

PREFACED BY SIR BARTLE FRERE.
Pandurang Hari.

BY EDWARD GARRETT.
The Capel Girls.

BY CHARLES GIBBON.
Robin Gray.
For Lack of Gold.
In Love and War.
What will the World Say?
For the King.
In Honour Bound.
Queen of the Meadow.
In Pastures Green.
The Flower of the Forest.
A Heart's Problem.
The Braes of Yarrow.
The Golden Shaft.
Of High Degree.

BY THOMAS HARDY.
Under the Greenwood Tree.

BY JULIAN HAWTHORNE.
Garth.
Ellice Quentin.
Sebastian Stroma.
Prince Saroni's Wife.
Dust.

BY SIR A. HELPS.
Ivan de Biron.

BY MRS. ALFRED HUNT.
Thornicroft's Model.
The Leaden Casket.
Self-Condemned.

BY JEAN INGELOW.
Fated to be Free.

BY HENRY JAMES, Jun.
Confidence.

BY HARRIETT JAY.
The Queen of Connaught.
The Dark Colleen.

BY HENRY KINGSLEY.
Number Seventeen.
Oakshott Castle.

PICCADILLY NOVELS, *continued*—

BY E. LYNN LINTON.
Patricia Kemball.
Atonement of Leam Dundas.
The World Well Lost.
Under which Lord?
With a Silken Thread.
The Rebel of the Family.
"My Love!"

BY HENRY W. LUCY.
Gideon Fleyce.

BY JUSTIN McCARTHY, M.P.
The Waterdale Neighbours.
My Enemy's Daughter.
Linley Rochford. | A Fair Saxon.
Dear Lady Disdain.
Miss Misanthrope.
Donna Quixote.
The Comet of a Season.

BY GEORGE MAC DONALD, LL.D.
Paul Faber, Surgeon.
Thomas Wingfold, Curate.

BY MRS. MACDONELL.
Quaker Cousins.

BY KATHARINE S. MACQUOID.
Lost Rose. | The Evil Eye.

BY FLORENCE MARRYAT.
Open! Sesame! | Written In Fire.

BY JEAN MIDDLEMASS.
Touch and Go.

BY D. CHRISTIE MURRAY.
Life's Atonement. | Coals of Fire.
Joseph's Coat. | Val Strange.
A Model Father. | Hearts.
By the Gate of the Sea.

BY MRS. OLIPHANT.
Whiteladies.

BY MARGARET A. PAUL
Gentle and Simple.

BY JAMES PAYN.
Lost Sir Massingberd.
Best of Husbands
Fallen Fortunes.
Halves.
Walter's Word.
What He Cost Her
Less Black than We're Painted.
By Proxy.
High Spirits.
Under One Roof.
Carlyon's Year.
Confidential Agent.
From Exile.
A Grape from a Thorn.
For Cash Only.
Kit: A Memory.

PICCADILLY NOVELS, *continued—*

BY E. C. PRICE.
Valentina.

BY CHARLES READE, D.C.L.
It Is Never Too Late to Mend.
Hard Cash. | Peg Woffington.
Christie Johnstone.
Griffith Gaunt.
The Double Marriage.
Love Me Little, Love Me Long.
Foul Play.
The Cloister and the Hearth.
The Course of True Love.
The Autobiography of a Thief.
Put Yourself In His Place.
A Terrible Temptation.
The Wandering Heir. | A Simpleton.
A Woman-Hater. | Readiana.

BY MRS. J. H. RIDDELL.
Her Mother's Darling.
Prince of Wales's Garden-Party.

BY F. W. ROBINSON.
Women are Strange.
The Hands of Justice.

BY JOHN SAUNDERS.
Bound to the Wheel.
Guy Waterman.
One Against the World.
The Lion In the Path.
The Two Dreamers.

PICCADILLY NOVELS, *continued—*

BY T. W. SPEIGHT.
The Mysteries of Heron Dyke.

BY R. A. STERNDALE.
The Afghan Knife.

BY BERTHA THOMAS.
Proud Maisie. | Cressida.
The Violin-Player.

BY ANTHONY TROLLOPE.
The Way we Live Now.
The American Senator.
Frau Frohmann.
Marion Fay.
Kept In the Dark
Mr. Scarborough's Family.

BY FRANCES E. TROLLOPE.
Like Ships upon the Sea.
Anne Furness.
Mabel's Progress.

BY T. A. TROLLOPE.
Diamond Cut Diamond.

BY IVAN TURGENIEFF AND OTHERS.
Stories from Foreign Novelists.

BY SARAH TYTLER.
What She Came Through.
The Bride's Pass.

BY J. S. WINTER.
Cavalry Life.
Regimental Legends.

CHEAP EDITIONS OF POPULAR NOVELS.

Post 8vo, Illustrated boards, 2s. each.

[WILKIE COLLINS's NOVELS and BESANT and RICE's NOVELS may also be had in cloth limp at 2s. 6d. *See, too, the* PICCADILLY NOVELS, *for Library Editions.*]

BY EDMOND ABOUT.
The Fellah.

BY HAMILTON AÏDÉ.
Carr of Carrlyon. | Confidences.

BY MRS. ALEXANDER.
Maid, Wife, or Widow?

BY SHELSLEY BEAUCHAMP.
Grantley Grange.

BY W. BESANT & JAMES RICE.
Ready-Money Mortiboy.
With Harp and Crown.
This Son of Vulcan.
My Little Girl.
The Case of Mr. Lucraft.

BY BESANT AND RICE, *continued—*
The Golden Butterfly.
By Celia's Arbour.
The Monks of Thelema.
'Twas In Trafalgar's Bay.
The Seamy Side.
The Ten Years' Tenant.
The Chaplain of the Fleet.

BY FREDERICK BOYLE.
Camp Notes. | Savage Life.

BY BRET HARTE.
An Heiress of Red Dog.
Gabriel Conroy.
The Luck of Roaring Camp.
Flip.

CHEAP POPULAR NOVELS, *continued—*

BY ROBERT BUCHANAN.
The Shadow of the Sword.
A Child of Nature.

BY MRS. BURNETT.
Surly Tim.

BY MRS. LOVETT CAMERON.
Deceivers Ever.
Juliet's Guardian.

BY MACLAREN COBBAN.
The Cure of Souls.

BY C. ALLSTON COLLINS.
The Bar Sinister.

BY WILKIE COLLINS.
Antonina.
Basil.
Hide and Seek.
The Dead Secret.
Queen of Hearts.
My Miscellanies.
The Woman in White.
The Moonstone.
Man and Wife.
Poor Miss Finch.
Miss or Mrs. ?
The New Magdalen.
The Frozen Deep.
The Law and the Lady.
The Two Destinies.
The Haunted Hotel.
The Fallen Leaves.
Jezebel's Daughter.
The Black Robe.

BY MORTIMER COLLINS.
Sweet Anne Page.
Transmigration.
From Midnight to Midnight.
A Fight with Fortune.

MORTIMER & FRANCES COLLINS.
Sweet and Twenty.
Frances.
Blacksmith and Scholar.
The Village Comedy.
You Play me False.

BY DUTTON COOK.
Leo.
Paul Foster's Daughter.

BY J. LEITH DERWENT.
Our Lady of Tears.

CHEAP POPULAR NOVELS, *continued—*

BY CHARLES DICKENS.
Sketches by Boz.
The Pickwick Papers.
Oliver Twist.
Nicholas Nickleby.

BY MRS. ANNIE EDWARDES.
A Point of Honour.
Archie Lovell.

BY M. BETHAM-EDWARDS.
Felicia.

BY EDWARD EGGLESTON.
Roxy.

BY PERCY FITZGERALD.
Bella Donna.
Never Forgotten.
The Second Mrs. Tillotson.
Polly.
Seventy-five Brooke Street.

BY ALBANY DE FONBLANQUE.
Filthy Lucre.

BY R. E. FRANCILLON.
Olympia.
Queen Cophetua.
One by One.

BY EDWARD GARRETT.
The Capel Girls.

BY CHARLES GIBBON.
Robin Gray.
For Lack of Gold.
What will the World Say ?
In Honour Bound.
The Dead Heart.
In Love and War.
For the King.
Queen of the Meadow.
In Pastures Green.

BY WILLIAM GILBERT.
Dr. Austin's Guests.
The Wizard of the Mountain.
James Duke.

BY JAMES GREENWOOD.
Dick Temple.

BY ANDREW HALLIDAY.
Every-Day Papers.

BY LADY DUFFUS HARDY.
Paul Wynter's Sacrifice.

BY THOMAS HARDY.
Under the Greenwood Tree.

CHEAP POPULAR NOVELS, *continued—*
BY JULIAN HAWTHORNE.
Garth.
Ellice Quentin.
Sebastian Strome.
BY SIR ARTHUR HELPS.
Ivan de Biron.
BY TOM HOOD.
A Golden Heart.
BY VICTOR HUGO.
The Hunchback of Notre Dame.
BY MRS. ALFRED HUNT.
Thornicroft's Model.
The Leaden Casket.
BY JEAN INGELOW.
Fated to be Free.
BY HENRY JAMES, Jun.
Confidence.
BY HARRIETT JAY.
The Dark Colleen.
The Queen of Connaught.
BY HENRY KINGSLEY.
Oakshott Castle.
Number Seventeen.
BY E. LYNN LINTON.
Patricia Kemball.
The Atonement of Leam Dundas.
The World Well Lost.
Under which Lord?
With a Silken Thread.
The Rebel of the Family.
"My Love!"
BY JUSTIN McCARTHY, M.P.
Dear Lady Disdain.
The Waterdale Neighbours.
My Enemy's Daughter.
A Fair Saxon.
Linley Rochford.
Miss Misanthrope.
Donna Quixote.
BY GEORGE MACDONALD.
Paul Faber, Surgeon.
Thomas Wingfold, Curate.
BY MRS. MACDONELL.
Quaker Cousins.
BY KATHARINE S. MACQUOID.
The Evil Eye. | Lost Rose.
BY W. H. MALLOCK.
The New Republic.

CHEAP POPULAR NOVELS, *continued—*
BY FLORENCE MARRYAT.
Open! Sesame!
A Harvest of Wild Oats.
A Little Stepson.
Fighting the Air.
Written in Fire.
BY JEAN MIDDLEMASS.
Touch and Go. | Mr. Dorillion.
BY D. CHRISTIE MURRAY.
A Life's Atonement.
A Model Father.
BY MRS. OLIPHANT.
Whiteladies.
BY MRS. ROBERT O'REILLY.
Phœbe's Fortunes.
BY OUIDA.
LIBRARY EDITIONS of OUIDA'S NOVELS may be had in crown 8vo, cloth extra, at 5s. each.
Held in Bondage. | Pascarel.
Strathmore. | TwoLittleWooden
Chandos. | Shoes.
Under Two Flags. | Signa.
Idalia. | In a Winter City.
Cecil Castle- | Ariadne.
  maine. | Friendship.
Tricotrin. | Moths.
Puck. | Pipistrello.
Folle Farine. | A Village Com-
A Dog of Flanders. | mune.
BY JAMES PAYN.
Lost Sir Massing- | Gwendoline's Har-
  berd. | vest.
A Perfect Trea- | Like Father, Like
  sure. | Son.
Bentinck's Tutor. | A Marine Resi-
Murphy's Master. | dence.
A County Family. | Married Beneath
At Her Mercy. | Him.
A Woman's Ven- | Mirk Abbey.
  geance. | Not Wooed, but
Cecil's Tryst. | Won.
Clyffards of Clyffe | £200 Reward.
The Family Scape- | Less Black than
  grace. | We're Painted.
Foster Brothers. | By Proxy.
Found Dead. | Under One Roof.
Best of Husbands | High Spirits.
Walter's Word. | Carlyon's Year.
Halves. | A Confidential
Fallen Fortunes. | Agent.
What He Cost Her | Some Private
Humorous Stories | Views. | From Exile.

CHEAP POPULAR NOVELS, continued—

BY EDGAR A. POE.
The Mystery of Marie Roget.

BY E. C. PRICE.
Valentina.

BY CHARLES READE.
It Is Never Too Late to Mend.
Hard Cash.
Peg Woffington.
Christie Johnstone.
Griffith Gaunt.
Put Yourself In His Place.
The Double Marriage.
Love Me Little, Love Me Long.
Foul Play.
The Cloister and the Hearth
The Course of True Love.
Autobiography of a Thief.
A Terrible Temptation.
The Wandering Heir.
A Simpleton.
A Woman-Hater.
Readiana.

BY MRS. RIDDELL.
Her Mother's Darling.

BY BAYLE ST. JOHN.
A Levantine Family.

BY GEORGE AUGUSTUS SALA.
Gaslight and Daylight.

BY JOHN SAUNDERS.
Bound to the Wheel.
One Against the World.
Guy Waterman.
The Lion In the Path.
The Two Dreamers.

BY ARTHUR SKETCHLEY.
A Match In the Dark.

BY T. W. SPEIGHT.
The Mysteries of Heron Dyke.

BY R. A. STERNDALE.
The Afghan Knife.

BY BERTHA THOMAS.
Cressida. | Proud Maisie
The Violin-Player.

CHEAP POPULAR NOVELS, continued—

BY WALTER THORNBURY.
Tales for the Marines.

BY T. ADOLPHUS TROLLOPE.
Diamond Cut Diamond.

BY ANTHONY TROLLOPE.
The Way We Live Now.
The American Senator.

BY MARK TWAIN.
Tom Sawyer.
An Idle Excursion.
A Pleasure Trip on the Continent
of Europe.

BY SARAH TYTLER.
What She Came Through.

BY LADY WOOD.
Sabina.

BY EDMUND YATES.
Castaway.
The Forlorn Hope.
Land at Last.

ANONYMOUS.
Paul Ferroll.
Why Paul Ferroll Killed his Wife.

Fcap. 8vo, picture covers, 1s. each.
Jeff Brigge's Love Story. By BRET
HARTE.
The Twins of Table Mountain. By
BRET HARTE.
Mrs. Gainsborough's Diamonds. By
JULIAN HAWTHORNE.
Kathleen Mavourneen. By Author
of "That Lass o' Lowrie's."
Lindsay's Luck. By the Author of
"That Lass o' Lowrie's."
Pretty Polly Pemberton. By the
Author of "That Lass o' Lowrie's."
Trooping with Crows. By Mrs.
PIRKIS.
The Professor's Wife. By LEONARD
GRAHAM.
A Double Bond. By LINDA VILLARI.
Esther's Glove. By R. E. FRANCILLON.
The Garden that Paid the Rent.
By TOM JERROLD.

J. OGDEN AND CO., PRINTERS, 172, ST. JOHN STREET, E.C.

CPSIA information can be obtained at www.ICGtesting.com
Printed in the USA
BVOW02s0015080616

451109BV00022B/298/P